Oxford Chemistry Series

General Editors
P. W. ATKINS   J. S. E. HOLKER   A. K. HOLLIDAY

Oxford Chemistry Series

1972

1. K. A. McLauchlan: *Magnetic resonance*
2. J. Robbins: *Ions in solution (2): an introduction to electrochemistry*
3. R. J. Puddephatt: *The periodic table of the elements*
4. R. A. Jackson: *Mechanism: an introduction to the study of organic reactions*

1973

5. D. Whittaker: *Stereochemistry and mechanism*
6. G. Hughes: *Radiation chemistry*
7. G. Pass: *Ions in solution (3): inorganic properties*
8. E. B. Smith: *Basic chemical thermodynamics*
9. C. A. Coulson: *The shape and structure of molecules*
10. J. Wormald: *Diffraction methods*
11. J. Shorter: *Correlation analysis in organic chemistry: an introduction to linear free-energy relationships*

GEOFFREY PASS

Ions in solution (3)

inorganic properties

Clarendon Press · Oxford · 1973

Oxford University Press, Ely House, London W.1

GLASGOW   NEW YORK   TORONTO   MELBOURNE   WELLINGTON
CAPE TOWN   IBADAN   NAIROBI   DAR ES SALAAM   LUSAKA   ADDIS ABABA
DELHI   BOMBAY   CALCUTTA   MADRAS   KARACHI   LAHORE   DACCA
KUALA LUMPUR   SINGAPORE   HONG KONG   TOKYO

PRINTED IN GREAT BRITAIN BY
J. W. ARROWSMITH LTD., BRISTOL, ENGLAND

Editor's foreword

INORGANIC ions in solution have been viewed quite differently by inorganic and physical chemists. For the inorganic chemist they are seen as having certain essential qualitative properties which he can use—colour, the ability to precipitate other ions, oxidizing or reducing power, and so on. The physical chemist sees them as charged species in a polar environment which (with many restrictions) may be treated quantitatively. The purpose of this book is to bring these two viewpoints together, so that the everyday reactions of inorganic ions in solution are, as far as possible, explained in physicochemical terms. Necessarily, the explanations are to some extent incomplete and empirical. Nevertheless, it is hoped that the reader will, after reading this book, appreciate that inorganic ions in solution behave, not in apparently idiosyncratic and unpredictable ways, but in a manner often depending essentially on such simple properties as size and charge (and therefore upon their position in the periodic table), and upon the nature of the solvent in which the reactions occur.

More detailed discussion of the structures of the water molecule and other species of interest will be found in C. A. Coulson's *The shape and structure of molecules* (OCS 9). The relevant thermodynamics can be found in E. B. Smith's *Basic chemical thermodynamics* (OCS 8). The use of electrical measurements is described in J. Robbins's *Ions in solution (2): an introduction to electrochemistry* (OCS 2); R. J. Puddephatt's *The periodic table of the elements* (OCS 3) provides the background of inorganic chemistry.

A.K.H.

Preface

INORGANIC chemistry is frequently concerned with the study of reactions in solution, especially aqueous solution, and my text has been prepared with this aspect of the subject in mind. First, consideration is given to the factors which govern the solubility of salts and the formation of ions in solution. However, the usefulness of the solvent is not confined to the production of a solution containing only the ions that were present in the original compound; different ions may be produced as a result of interactions with the solvent or with other ions in the solution. This is the next topic to be discussed.

Succeeding chapters describe the reactions of the ions of the various groups of elements in the periodic table. The behaviour of the compounds is treated in terms of an ionic model, and the factors leading to deviations from this model are discussed. A detailed account of the solution chemistry of the elements has not been attempted, but the main features of the chemistry of each group are used to illustrate the trends within the periodic table. The aim is to establish a pattern of behaviour within which the chemistry of a given element will be more clearly understood.

The elements which adhere closely to the ionic model are treated first, then the elements which show marked deviations from the model, followed by the transition elements which exhibit progressive changes in behaviour. The discussion is completed with an outline of the solution chemistry of the non-metals. The chemistry is considered in terms of soluble and insoluble compounds, the effect of changes in the acidity of the solution, the stability of the compounds with respect to oxidation or reduction, and the formation of complex ions. The final chapter describes the reactions of ions in solution as applied in qualitative analysis and in oxidation and reduction reactions.

The book is designed primarily for use as part of the lecture programme in the early years of a degree course in chemistry, but it may also be used as an information source for the laboratory investigation of solution reactions on a test-tube scale; an aspect of the subject on which increasing emphasis is being placed.

Department of Chemistry,   G. PASS
University of Salford

Contents

1. SOLVENTS AND SOLUTIONS   1

Properties of ionizing solvents. Solute–solvent interactions. Solvated ions. Solvent effects. Solvent structure.

2. THE PROCESS OF SOLUTION   11

Enthalpy and entropy changes. Relative permittivity. Hydrate formation. Solubility product. Polarization effects. Solution of covalent molecules.

3. EQUILIBRIUM REACTIONS IN SOLUTION   20

Hydrolysis. Complex-ion formation. Electrode potentials.

4. ACIDS AND BASES   27

Buffer solutions. Complex cations as acids. Acidic and basic oxides. Polyanions. Amphoteric oxides. Polarization effects.

5. THE ELEMENTS OF GROUP IA AND GROUP IIA   37

Group IA. Group IIA.

6. THE ELEMENTS OF GROUP IIIA, THE LANTHANIDES, AND THE ACTINIDES   46

Electronic configuration. Solubility and hydrolysis. Complex ions. Separation of lanthanides and actinides. Oxidation states other than $+3$.

7. THE METALS OF THE B-SUBGROUPS   53

Electronic configuration. Polarization effects. Complex ions. Group IIB: zinc, cadmium, and mercury. Group IIIB: gallium, indium, and thallium. Group IVB: germanium, tin, and lead. Group VB: arsenic, antimony, and bismuth.

8. THE TRANSITION METALS   63

Electronic configuration. d-orbital splitting. Oxidation states. Standard electrode potentials. Ion size. Hydrolysis. Solubility. Complex ions. Stereochemistry. Oxo-cations. Oxo-anions.

9. THE NON-METALS   77

Ionic species. Acid properties. Boron. Group IVB: carbon, silicon, and germanium. Group VB: nitrogen, phosphorus, and arsenic. Group VIB: oxygen, sulphur, selenium, and tellurium. Group VIIB: fluorine, chlorine, bromine, and iodine. Solvated electrons.

10. REACTIONS OF IONS IN SOLUTION   88

Group separations. The mechanism of oxidation and reduction.

BIBLIOGRAPHY   98

INDEX   99

1. Solvents and solutions

Properties of ionizing solvents

THE consideration of ions in solution may usefully begin with an examination of the properties of solvents which commonly produce solutions containing ions. Water is readily available, and dissolves a wide range of compounds, so it is not surprising that most of the work on solution chemistry, at least inorganic chemistry, has been done using water as solvent. The position of water is so dominant that solvents are usually divided into two categories, aqueous and non-aqueous solvents.

The water molecule in the vapour state is non-linear, with an H—O—H bond angle of 105°.† The O—H bond is polar, because the two atoms have different electronegativities, and the shape of the molecule does not eliminate the polar effects of the individual bonds, as would be the case for a linear molecule. The charge distribution within the molecule is such that positive charge is concentrated in the region between the hydrogen atoms and negative charge is concentrated on the oxygen atom. This produces a dipole moment for the water molecule of $6 \cdot 1 \times 10^{-30}$ C m. One consequence of the polar nature of the molecules is the relatively high value of the permittivity of liquid water.

As a result of the polarity of the molecules there is strong intermolecular association in the liquid. This takes the form of *hydrogen bonding* between the positively-charged hydrogen of one water molecule and the negatively-charged oxygen of another. The geometry of the molecule is such that a three-dimensional network of hydrogen bonds is produced within the liquid. The liquid is therefore highly associated, and has a higher boiling point and entropy of vaporization than expected by comparison with the hydrides of the other group VIB elements. Hydrogen bonding is essentially electrostatic in nature, and its strength is governed by the charge separation in the individual molecules. This in turn depends on the difference between the electronegativities of the two atoms in the bond. For a bond H—A the electronegativity of A decreases down the group, and the high degree of association of water compared with hydrogen sulphide reflects the difference in the polarities of the molecules. Ammonia and hydrogen fluoride are also polar molecules which are highly associated in the liquid phase, although the geometry of the molecules prevents the formation of a three-dimensional network as found in water. Again the boiling points are higher than expected compared with the corresponding hydrides of the lower elements of each group, and both compounds find considerable application as ionizing solvents. See Fig. 1.

† The shape of the water molecule, and the others mentioned below, is discussed by C. A. Coulson in *The shape and structure of molecules* (OCS 9).

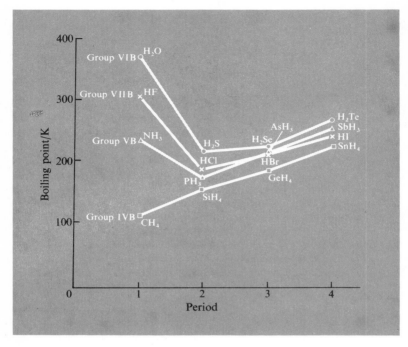

FIG. 1. The boiling points of selected hydrides.

Historically, the suggestion that ions were present in aqueous solution was first made to explain the results of electrolysis. Now the general view is that certain compounds dissociate completely into ions in dilute solutions. Such compounds are termed *strong electrolytes*. Other compounds, which are called *weak electrolytes*, are only partially dissociated into ions even in dilute solution. However, a given ion X^- behaves in an identical manner whether it is obtained from a strong electrolyte AX or from a weak electrolyte BX. With increasing concentration the situation becomes less clear-cut, even for a strong electrolyte, and consideration has to be given to the possibility of interaction between ions of opposite charge and to the effects of the ions on the properties of the solvent.

Solute–solvent interactions

When a covalent molecule, such as a hydrocarbon, dissolves in a non-polar solvent such as benzene, the relatively weak intermolecular forces between the solute molecules are replaced by weak solute–solvent interactions. The increased entropy achieved by the solute molecules is mainly responsible for the dissolving of the solute. Because solution arises from an entropy effect,† solubility usually increases markedly with increasing temperature as a result of the $-T\Delta S$ term in the free energy of dissolution (see p. 11). In non-polar solvents, although the intermolecular attractive forces between solvent molecules are relatively small, an ionic compound will have little solubility because the solvent–solute interaction is insufficient to overcome the strong electrostatic binding energy of the crystal lattice.

The interaction between solute and solvent must be substantial if ions are to be produced in the solution. Considerable energy (between 200 and 400 kJ mol^{-1}) is required to overcome the electrostatic forces which bind an ionic crystal lattice, or to produce heterolytic fission of a covalent bond. Furthermore, many ionizing solvents are associated liquids, and if production of ions in the solution involves disruption of this structure then additional energy will be required. The *solvation energy* is the energy released by the interaction between the gaseous ion and the solvent molecules, that is by the process

$$A^{n\pm}(g) \; + \; \text{solvent} \quad \rightarrow \quad A^{n\pm}\,\text{(solvated)}$$

The net energy change will be a small difference between the two large energy terms.

The generally accepted model for an ion in solution assumes that there is a close layer of solvent molecules in which the solvent dipoles are oriented by the ionic charge. The solvent molecules in this first sphere or *coordination sphere*—also called the *inner sphere*—are attached to the central ion by ion–dipole forces or coordinate bonds. This coordination sphere is surrounded by other layers of solvent molecules, interacting progressively less strongly, until at some distance from the ion the solvent molecules are under the same influence as in the pure solvent. The interactions in the coordination sphere will be stronger the smaller the ion and the higher the dipole moment of the solvent molecule. Thus solvation energies of cations are usually greater than solvation energies of anions, because cations are usually smaller.‡ The solvation energy of M^{n+} in water is approximately equal (but opposite in sign) to the total ionization potential for $M \rightarrow M^{n+}$. This corresponds to the exothermic recombination reaction of n electrons with the gaseous ion, and indicates that the water molecule transfers considerable electron density to the metal ion. The process of ionization is enhanced by solvation of the anion; when the solvent molecules possess polar hydrogen atoms, hydrogen bonding leads to strong interaction with suitable anions (e.g. F^-, Cl^-, and many oxo-anions such as SO_4^{2-}); water is a solvent of this kind.

† The role of entropy and free energy in the dissolution process is discussed by E. B. Smith in *Basic chemical thermodynamics* (OCS 8).

‡ The sizes of atoms and ions are discussed by R. J. Puddephatt in *The periodic table of the elements* (OCS 3).

When a covalent molecule dissolves in an ionizing solvent with the formation of ions a possible preliminary step involves incipient transfer of electrons from the solvent to the covalent molecule. This changes the electron distribution in the covalent bond;

$$S + A{-}B \rightarrow \overset{\frown}{S} \overset{\rightarrow}{} A{-}B \rightarrow (S{-}A)^+ \ B^-$$

The greater the donor properties of the solvent the more electron density will be transferred from A to B. If electron transfer from A to B is complete, heterolytic fission of the bond A—B will occur and ions will be produced. The ionization step is facilitated if the cation is stabilized by coordination and if the solvent can solvate the anion. As a result of the electron transfer between solvent and solute, associated ions are produced, and the once-covalent solute is now comparable to the ionic crystal. The separation of the ions in the solution will depend on the permittivity of the medium, since the force of interaction F between two charges $+q_1$ and $-q_2$ is given by

$$F = \frac{q_1 q_2}{4\pi\varepsilon r^2}$$

where ε is the permittivity of the medium and r is the distance between the charges. Some physical properties of selected solvents are listed in Table 1.

TABLE 1

Physical properties of some solvents

	H_2O	NH_3	HF	H_2SO_4
Melting point/K	273·1	195·4	183·7	284·5
Boiling point/K	373·1	239·7	292·6	563·4
Relative permittivity $\varepsilon/\varepsilon_0$ (or dielectric constant D)	78·5	23	84	100
Electrolytic conductivity ($\Omega^{-1}\,m^{-1}$)	$\sim 5 \times 10^{-5}$	$\sim 10^{-9}$	$\sim 10^{-4}$	1·04
Dipole moment (C m)	$6 \cdot 1 \times 10^{-30}$	$4 \cdot 8 \times 10^{-30}$	$6 \cdot 0 \times 10^{-30}$	—
Density (kg m^{-3})	$1 \cdot 0 \times 10^3$	$0 \cdot 69 \times 10^3$	$1 \cdot 0 \times 10^3$	$1 \cdot 83 \times 10^3$

Solvated ions

Experimental evidence shows that an ion in solution is associated with a definite number of water molecules in the coordination sphere. Isotopic-dilution experiments in which $H_2^{18}O$ is added to an aqueous solution containing $Cr(III)$ or $Al(III)$ ions have been interpreted in terms of instantaneous mixing of the $H_2^{18}O$ with all the solvent except six molecules of water per cation. The $Co(II)$ cation forms a solid aquo-complex $Co(ClO_4)_2 \cdot 6H_2O$ which is shown by X-ray diffraction to have an octahedral array of water molecules around the Co(II) ion. The spectroscopic properties of aqueous solutions of Co(II) are identical with those of the Co(II) in the solid hydrate. This strongly suggests that aquo-ions contain a definite number of water molecules with a fixed stereochemistry, and that an aquo-ion such as $Cr(H_2O)_6^{3+}$ is as real a species as $Cr(NH_3)_6^{3+}$ or $Cr(CN)_6^{3-}$.

The interaction between the ion and the solvent increases with decreasing size of the ion. The interaction between the proton and solvents is therefore of interest because of the very small size of the free proton. A large interaction with a polar solvent such as water would be expected, and an absolute value of -1091 kJ mol^{-1} has been given for the heat of hydration of the proton. The proton affinity for water vapour is approximately -760 kJ mol^{-1}, which means that the heat of reaction for $H_3O^+(g) \rightarrow H_3O^+(aq)$ is approximately -330 kJ mol^{-1}. As with the Cr^{3+} ion there is evidence that at ordinary concentrations the *hydronium ion* (H_3O^+) is bound to a definite number of water molecules. Three water molecules are attached, with each hydrogen atom in H_3O^+ hydrogen-bonded to the oxygen atom of a water molecule, giving the species $H_9O_4^+$. Similarly, the hydroxide ion is bound to three water molecules giving the species $H_7O_4^-$. Possible structures for the $H_9O_4^+$ and $H_7O_4^-$ ions are shown in Fig. 2.

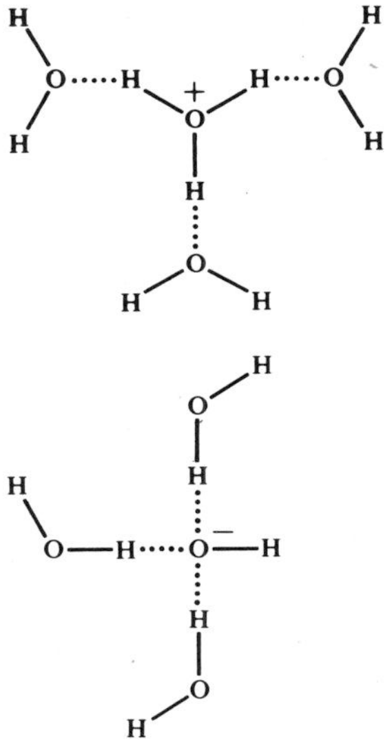

FIG. 2. Possible structures of $H_9O_4^+$ and $H_7O_4^-$.

Solvent effects

Further insight into the effects of dipole moment and permittivity may be obtained by comparing the behaviour of ionic solutes in water and in some other polar solvent in which these two properties are different, such as liquid ammonia. Solubilities are usually lower in liquid ammonia than in water, but the general pattern of solubilities remains essentially unchanged. Thus many salts are soluble in liquid ammonia, but organic molecules will dissolve if hydrogen-bond formation with the solvent can occur. The generally lower solubilities of ionic compounds are consistent with the lower dipole moment and permittivity of liquid ammonia.

One effect of transferring a strong electrolyte (such as potassium bromide) from water to a solvent of low permittivity is an increase in ion association, with the formation of ion pairs (A^+B^-), ion triplets $(A^+B^-A^+)$ and $(B^-A^+B^-)$, and ion quadruplets $(A^+B^-A^+B^-)$ or $\begin{pmatrix} A^+B^- \\ B^-A^+ \end{pmatrix}$. In glacial acetic acid $(\varepsilon_r = 6.2)$ the ion-pair dissociation constant for the reaction $(K^+Br^-) \rightleftharpoons K^+ + Br^-$ is 1×10^{-7} mol dm^{-3}. The variation of conductivity with concentration of solutions of potassium bromide in liquid ammonia is attributed to the formation of ion triplets $(Br^-K^+Br^-)$.

The change from one solvent to another will inevitably change physical properties other than dipole moment and permittivity, so it is not surprising to find effects due to changes in other properties of the solvent. For example, the ammonia molecule is more *polarizable* than the water molecule, and in certain cases the *ion–induced-dipole* interaction makes a significant contribution to the solvation energy. A molecule or an ion is polarizable if its electron cloud is distorted by the presence of a neighbouring ion. Large molecules are generally more polarizable than small ones, and cations are usually smaller and less polarizable than anions. The presence of an ion, especially a cation, in a solvent, induces dipoles in neighbouring solvent molecules by polarization. This ion–induced-dipole contribution is in addition to any interaction with the permanent dipole on the solvent molecule. The smaller or more highly-charged the cation the greater will be its polarizing power, and the greater will be the ion–induced-dipole interactions. In certain cases this ion–induced-dipole interaction will be sufficient to overcome the increase in lattice energy also associated with small size and high charge, and leads to increased solubility. Thus lithium salts are more soluble than the other alkali-metal salts in liquid ammonia, but usually less soluble than the other alkali-metal salts in water.

Although ammonia has stronger donor properties than water (towards some cations), it is less effective in solvating anions. Thus decreasing size and increasing charge of the anion lead to increased lattice energy, but there is no compensating increase in anion–solvent interaction. The solubility will depend primarily on whether the cation solvation energy can overcome the lattice energy. This is most likely to occur when a readily-solvated cation is associated with a large anion in the ionic solute. Thus silver ions are strongly polarizing and silver iodide is insoluble in water because the polarization of the iodide ion leads to a high lattice energy. However the silver cation interacts more strongly with the polarizable ammonia molecule. The solvation energy is now greater than the lattice energy and the compound can therefore dissolve both in concentrated aqueous ammonia and in liquid ammonia.

TABLE 2

Solubilities of selected salts in liquid ammonia and in water (mol dm^{-3})

Salt	$LiNO_3$	$NaNO_3$	KNO_3	$AgNO_3$	KI	AgI
Solubility in water	7·5	10·7	3·8	14·2	8·9	$1·2 \times 10^{-8}$
Solubility in ammonia	23·5	7·7	0·7	3·3	7·5	5·9

One further result of changing the solvent is that the ionic species produced in the solution from a given solute may be changed considerably. A few examples will show the effects that may occur. A metal nitrate dissolved in water will produce metal ions and nitrate ions, but in sulphuric acid the nitronium ion NO_2^+ is produced,

$$NO_3^- + 3H_2SO_4 \rightarrow NO_2^+ + H_3O^+ + 3HSO_4^-.$$

In water acetic acid dissociates into the acetate ion and the hydronium ion, but in sulphuric acid it is protonated and $CH_3C(OH)_2^+$ and HSO_4^- ions are present:

$$CH_3 \cdot C{\overset{O}{\underset{OH}{\big\langle}}} + H_2SO_4 \rightarrow CH_3 \cdot C^+{\overset{OH}{\underset{OH}{\big\langle}}} + HSO_4^-$$

Perhaps one of the more remarkable changes involves the alkali metals. An alkali metal dissolves in water with the liberation of hydrogen and produces M^+ and OH^- ions. In pure dry liquid ammonia the metal dissolves without liberation of hydrogen, producing the metal ion and a solvated electron.

Ions in solution will always be surrounded by solvent molecules (p. 3). Ions in aqueous solution may be represented as $[M(H_2O)_x]^{n+}$ where reference is made to the coordination sphere only. Since this aquo-ion is associated with other water molecules it may be represented in general terms as M^{n+}(aq).

Solvent Structure

So far we have considered the effect of the solvent on the solute, but now some attention will be given to the effect of the ions on the structure of the solvent. The structures of liquids are not well understood, and we shall confine our attention to water, since it is the solvent of major interest, and the solvent for which most information is available.

The structure of ice has been shown by X-ray diffraction to consist of a tetrahedral array of oxygen atoms. This can be understood in terms of a tetrahedral distribution of the two lone pairs and the two hydrogen atoms

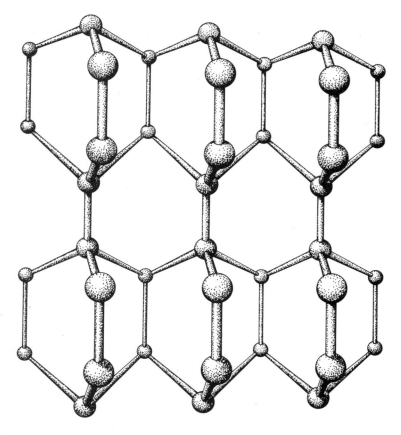

FIG. 3. Structure of ice, showing the tetrahedral configuration of oxygen atoms. Each oxygen is linked to four others by hydrogen bonds.

about each oxygen atom. In the tetrahedral unit the central oxygen atom is hydrogen-bonded to the oxygen atoms at the corners; this produces a three-dimensional structure.

Several models have been proposed for the structure of water which are closely related to the structure of ice. One suggestion is that the hydrogen bonds are distorted but not broken, and the linked networks of water molecules are irregular and varied in contrast to the orderly array in ice. An alternative view is that some hydrogen bonds are broken, so that the liquid consists of a mixture of separate molecules and hydrogen-bonded species that are different from the hydrogen-bonded species in ice.

When a noble gas dissolves, the entropy of solution is negative for a non-polar solvent, but still more negative for a polar solvent. The noble-gas atom loses freedom of movement in going from the gas phase to the solution and so there is a decrease in entropy. In a polar solvent such as water the noble-gas atom not only loses freedom of movement but also produces ordering of solvent molecules around it. This further ordering of the system is responsible for the greater loss of entropy in polar solvents. In addition to this structure-making process there will be a structure-breaking effect on the more distant water molecules, since the newly-formed structure will not fit easily into the existing water structure. Beyond this region of re-ordered water molecules there will be a region of unchanged water structure. Such an arrangement is of course similar to the model proposed for the solvation of an ion (p. 3). The entropy decrease produced when a gaseous ion dissolves is less than the entropy decrease produced by a noble-gas atom of the same size. This suggests that the structure-breaking effects of ions are greater than those of noble-gas atoms, since structure breaking corresponds to increase of entropy.

The effect of an ion on the water structure depends on its size and charge. Small or highly-charged cations produce a net increase in structure, but with some larger cations there may be a decrease in structure. Fluoride ion produces a net increase in structure, but the other halide ions are structure-breaking. Oxo-anions also show a range of properties; nitrate decreases the structure in the solution but carbonate increases it.

A similar type of structural ordering is expected for other polar solvents, but non-polar solvents are not structured in the same way. The structuring of polar solvents is due to attractive forces between oppositely-orientated dipoles, but any structure in non-polar solvents will arise from the combined effects of repulsion of like atoms and weak Van der Waals interactions.

PROBLEMS

1.1. Draw a model of an ion with its surrounding solvent molecules.
1.2. Describe briefly the evidence supporting the existence of ions in solution.

1.3. What is the shape of the ammonia molecule? Show that ammonia molecules cannot form as extensive a structure as water molecules in the liquid phase.

1.4. Explain why ionic solutes are more soluble in polar than in non-polar solvents.

1.5. Lithium nitrate is more soluble in liquid ammonia than in water, but potassium nitrate is less soluble. Explain these observations.

2. The process of solution

THE fact that ionic solids will dissolve in polar solvents is a result of the inter-actions between the ions and the solvent molecules. A study of the energy changes involved in such interactions provides useful information about the possible solubility of a solute in a solvent. We shall confine our attention to aqueous solutions, for which most information is available.

Enthalpy and entropy changes

At constant temperature and pressure the net energy change occurring on solution (that is, the change in the Gibbs free energy)† can be considered in terms of the energy cycle

$$
\begin{array}{ccc}
& & A^+(g) \ + \ B^-(g) \\
& (1)\nearrow & \\
AB(s) & & (2)\downarrow \\
& (3)\searrow & \\
& & A^+(aq) \ + \ B^-(aq)
\end{array}
$$

The change in the free energy ΔG is related to the change in enthalpy ΔH and the change in entropy ΔS by the expression $\Delta G = \Delta H - T\Delta S$. Consequently the changes occurring in the energy cycle may be discussed in terms of an enthalpy change and an entropy change. For either the enthalpy or the entropy change, the total change represented by (3) must be equal to the sum of the changes in stages (1) and (2).

Enthalpy of solution

The enthalpy change for reaction (1), the energy needed to break the crystal lattice and separate the gaseous ions, is called the *lattice energy* of the solid, U_L, and is a positive or endothermic energy term (the lattice is energetically more stable than a gas of ions). The enthalpy change for reaction (3) is the *heat of solution*, which can be measured experimentally. Thus the total heat of hydration of the cation plus the anion is $\Delta H_{hydrn} = \Delta H_{soln} - U_L$. At this stage the calculated heat of hydration is for both ions together, and although it seems reasonable to assume that this is made up of the hydration enthalpies of the individual ions no assignment of the distribution of the total energy between the individual ions can be made. However, if the value for any one ion is established then the values for all ions may be calculated by using a

---

† The role of the Gibbs free energy in chemistry is described by E. B. Smith in *Basic chemical thermodynamics* (OCS 8).

suitable series of electrolytes with ions in common. The hydration enthalpy of the proton has been estimated as 1091 kJ mol^{-1} and this allows hydration enthalpies of other cations and anions to be calculated.

Entropy of solution

Referring again to the energy cycle (p. 11), the total entropy of the ions in solution $\{S_{A^+}(\text{aq}) + S_{B^-}(\text{aq})\}$ will be the sum of the entropy of the solid AB (S_{AB}) and the entropy change occurring when the solid dissolves (ΔS_{soln}). Both these terms can be measured experimentally. The entropies of the individual gaseous ions A^+ and B^- can be calculated by the normal techniques of statistical thermodynamics and the entropy sum for the gaseous ions will be $S_{A^+}(\text{g}) + S_{B^-}(\text{g})$. The entropy of hydration for the sum of $A^+ + B^-$ ions, step 2, will be given by

$$\Delta S_{\text{hydrn}} = \{S_{A^+}(\text{aq}) + S_{B^-}(\text{aq})\} - \{S_{A^+}(\text{g}) + S_{B^-}(\text{g})\}.$$

Single-ion values may be obtained by adopting the *convention* that the entropy of $H^+(\text{aq})$ is zero. The overall entropy change ΔS for the reaction

$$A(\text{s}) + H^+(\text{aq}) \rightarrow A^+(\text{aq}) + \tfrac{1}{2}H_2(\text{g})$$

is calculated from the experimentally determined free-energy and enthalpy changes. Since the entropies of $A(\text{s})$ and $H_2(\text{g})$ are known, and the entropy of $H^+(\text{aq})$ is arbitrarily taken as zero, then the entropy of $A^+(\text{aq})$ relative to $H^+(\text{aq})$ can be calculated. The entropy of hydration is the difference between the entropy of the ion in solution $S_{A^+}(\text{aq})$ and in the gas phase $S_{A^+}(\text{g})$; but remember that these entropies are *relative* entropies, and that the *absolute* entropies can be found only if the *absolute* entropy of $H^+(\text{aq})$ can be found.

The entropy of hydration will depend to some extent on the ordering produced in the solution and is part of the evidence adduced to support the designation of ions as structure-forming or structure-breaking. Thus the hydration entropies of the halides become less negative from F^- to I^- and from Li^+ to Cs^+, as shown in Table 3.

TABLE 3

Entropies of selected ions ($J \ K^{-1} \text{ mol}^{-1}$ at 298 K)

	Li^+	Na^+	K^+	Rb^+	Cs^+	Ag^+	F^-	Cl^-	Br^-	I^-
$S(\text{aq})$	14·2	60·3	102·5	124·3	133·1	74·1	−9·6	55·2	80·1	109·2
$S(\text{g})$	133·1	147·7	154·4	164·5	169·9	168·0	145·6	152·0	164·0	170·0
$S(\text{s})$	14·6	31·4	38·5	49·8	42·7	50·5	23·0	41·9	54·4	61·1

The free energy of solvation of an ion may be calculated directly from the *Born equation*

$$\Delta G^{\ominus} = -\frac{Lz^2e^2}{8\pi\varepsilon_0 r}\left(1 - \frac{1}{\varepsilon_r}\right)$$

where L = the Avogadro constant = 6.022×10^{23} mol^{-1}
z = the numerical value of the charge on the ion, 1, 2, ...
e = the magnitude of the electronic charge = 1.602×10^{-19} C
r = the radius of the ion
ε_0 = the permittivity of a vacuum = 8.854×10^{-12} F m^{-1}
ε = the permittivity of the solvent

$\varepsilon_r = \dfrac{\varepsilon}{\varepsilon_0}$ = the relative permittivity (also called dielectric constant)

Expressions for the hydration enthalpy and hydration entropy may be derived from this equation, which on substitution reduce to

$$\Delta H^{\ominus} = -69.9 \times \frac{10^3 z^2}{r}\text{ nm J mol}^{-1} \qquad \Delta S^{\ominus} = -4.10 \times \frac{z^2}{r}\text{ nm J K}^{-1}\text{ mol}^{-1}$$

Good agreement between measured and calculated values for cation-plus-anion hydration enthalpies is obtained if the radii of aquated cations are assumed to be 0.085 nm greater than the crystal radii, and those of aquated anions 0.01 nm greater. Using these empirical radii, values for the enthalpies of hydration of single ions can be obtained.

The single-ion values for hydration enthalpy and entropy show a number of trends. Small size and high charge favour high values of hydration enthalpy. Thus for $+1$, $+2$, and $+3$ ions of approximately the same size the enthalpies of hydration are Li$^+$ -519 kJ mol^{-1}, Mg^{2+} -1921 kJ mol^{-1}, and Fe^{3+} -4430 kJ mol^{-1}. The enthalpy is approximately proportional to the square of the charge, in keeping with the Born equation. The enthalpies also decrease for constant charge and increasing radius. The overall heat of solution is a small difference between two large terms; the total hydration enthalpy and the lattice energy. Thus relatively small changes in either the enthalpy of hydration or the lattice energy can produce a significant change in the heat of solution.

For cations of similar size there are corresponding trends for the hydration entropies with Li$^+$, Mg^{2+}, and Fe^{3+} ions having entropies of approximately -120, -270, and -460 J K^{-1} mol^{-1} respectively. Entropies apparently depend more than enthalpies on changes in radius and on the sign of the charge. Thus entropy terms favour the solubility of salts containing large ions of low charge.

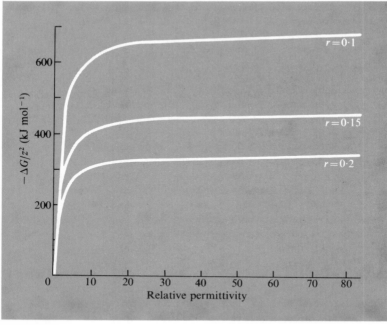

FIG. 4. Plot of free-energy change occurring on solvation in solvents of different relative permittivity; r/nm is the ion size, z is the absolute value of the ionic charge in M^{z+}.

Relative permittivity

The effect of the relative permittivity on the free energy of solvation of ions can also be calculated from the Born equation. The large solvation energy of small cations means that compounds containing small cations and large anions, where the lattice energy is low, will have appreciable solubility in solvents with quite low relative permittivities. As shown in Fig. 4, the increase in solvation energy with relative permittivity is quite small above a relative permittivity of about 30, so that all solvents with relative permittivities above 30 might be expected to act as ionizing solvents.

Hydrate formation

The formation of a hydrated salt is an indication of high solubility for the anhydrous compound. If a hydrated salt is obtained from solution this must mean that it is more stable than separate anhydrous salt and water, and that the hydrated salt is less soluble than the anhydrous salt. Compared with the anhydrous salt there must be a decrease in entropy in the formation of the hydrated salt since water molecules are fixed in the crystal lattice. Therefore the enthalpy change on solution must be larger and this indicates strong interaction between the ions and the solvent molecules. When a hydrate dissolves, the presence in the lattice of solvent molecules with high relative permittivity reduces the attractive force between the anion and the cation and hence, in solution, the ions of the lattice will separate more easily. It follows from the enthalpy and entropy changes occurring on the formation of the hydrated salt that when a hydrated salt dissolves there is a less favourable enthalpy change and a more favourable entropy change than when the anhydrous salt dissolves.

The position of the solution equilibrium will change with temperature; for a solution reaction with a positive enthalpy change the solubility of the salt should increase with increasing temperature. Thus the hydrated salt becomes more soluble relative to the anhydrous salt with increasing temperature, and a less dehydrated salt or the anhydrous salt may be the solid phase in equilibrium with the aquated ions at higher temperature.

Solubility product

When the solubility of the compound AB is very small, and undissolved solid is present, the equilibrium for the solution reaction may be written

$$AB(s) + H_2O \rightleftharpoons A^+(aq) + B^-(aq)$$

The equilibrium constant is given by

$$K = \frac{a_{A^+(aq)} a_{B^-(aq)}}{a_{AB(s)} a_{H_2O}}$$

where the a_X represent activities.† However, AB is present as solid and will have unit activity. Because the solubility is very small and the solution very dilute the activity of the water may be taken as the activity of pure water and equal to unity, and the activities of the ions will be almost equal to their concentrations, c_X. We may now write the expression as $K_{sp} = c^2$, where c is the concentration of $A^+(aq)$, which is equal to the concentration of $B^-(aq)$; K_{sp} is the *solubility product*. The free-energy change involved in the solution of a sparingly soluble compound AB is related to K_{sp} by $\Delta G^\ominus = -2.303 \, RT \lg K_{sp}$.‡ The free-energy change contains an enthalpy and an entropy term

·† Activities are a device for extending thermodynamic calculations to 'non-ideal' systems where the thermodynamic properties are not simply proportional to the amount of substance present. The definition and role of activities are discussed by E. B. Smith in *Basic chemical thermodynamics* (OCS 8), and their calculation for ionic solutions and application to the thermodynamic properties of ions in solution are described by J. Robbins in *Ions in solution* (2): *an introduction to electrochemistry* (OCS 2).

‡ We use the convention that $\lg x = \log_{10} x$ and $\ln x = \log_e x$.

given by $\Delta G^{\ominus} = \Delta H^{\ominus} - T\Delta S^{\ominus}$. The enthalpy corresponds to the enthalpy change in removing an ion from the lattice and placing it within its sphere of associated water molecules; the entropy term corresponds to the change in the order of the system when the ion is removed from its lattice and rearranges the solvent structure. The position of equilibrium will depend upon both these terms, so that a solute with an unfavourable enthalpy of solution (that is, an endothermic solution process) may still dissolve because of a favourable change in the entropy.

The solubility-product expression is true only for dilute solutions. Concentrated solutions of electrolytes are not ideal solutions and the simple equilibrium-constant expression in terms of concentrations does not apply. This means that we can distinguish between soluble and sparingly soluble salts, but once having decided that a salt is soluble we cannot use the above expression to calculate the concentration of a solution such as saturated potassium chloride.

We can use the solubility-product expression to demonstrate what effect the entropy of aqueous ions may have on the solution reaction. When lithium fluoride dissolves, the entropy of the system decreases because of the large ordering effect of the small ions. If an insoluble salt is arbitrarily defined as one that has a solubility less than 0·05 M then for a salt AB the limiting value of the free-energy change at 298 K is,

$$\Delta G^{\ominus} = -2\cdot303 \times 8\cdot314 \times 298 \lg 2\cdot5 \times 10^{-3} = 14\cdot8 \text{ kJ mol}^{-1}$$

For lithium fluoride the entropy change is

$$\text{LiF(s)} \rightarrow \text{Li}^{+}\text{(aq)} + \text{F}^{-}\text{(aq)}$$

| 37·6 | 14·2 − 9·6 | $\Delta S^{\ominus} = -33 \text{ J K}^{-1} \text{ mol}^{-1}$ |

and the limiting enthalpy change is

$$\Delta H^{\ominus} = 14\cdot8 - 9\cdot8 = 5\cdot0 \text{ kJ mol}^{-1}$$

Thus if the heat of solution of lithium fluoride is $\geqslant 5\cdot0$ kJ mol^{-1} then lithium fluoride will be 'insoluble' on this definition. Although the hydration enthalpies of these ions will be large there is also a large lattice energy to be overcome and the observed heat of solution of lithium fluoride is 4·31 kJ mol^{-1}. An 0·05 M lithium fluoride solution is approximately a saturated solution.

A generalization commonly made is that 'all metal nitrates are soluble'; this widespread solubility of the metal nitrates may be attributed in part to the large entropy of the aqueous nitrate ion. The effect may be shown by reference to lithium nitrate,

$$\text{LiNO}_3\text{(s)} \rightarrow \text{Li}^{+}\text{(aq)} + \text{NO}_3^{-}\text{(aq)}$$

| 105·4 | 14·2 + 146·5 | $\Delta S = 55\cdot3 \text{ J K}^{-1} \text{ mol}^{-1}$ |

and the limiting enthalpy change is

$$\Delta H = 14 \cdot 8 + 16 \cdot 5 = 31 \cdot 3 \text{ kJ mol}^{-1}$$

This is appreciably greater than the measured heat of solution of lithium nitrate, $-1 \cdot 8$ kJ mol^{-1}, and so the concentration of a saturated solution of lithium nitrate will be considerably greater than $0 \cdot 05$ M.

Polarization effects

One factor which affects the lattice energy of a salt, and consequently its solubility, is an interaction between the cation and anion giving rise to partial covalent character in the crystal. This effect is termed *polarization*. The crystal radii of K^+ and Ag^+ are $0 \cdot 133$ nm and $0 \cdot 126$ nm respectively, but comparison of the solubilities of their halides in water shows that although the fluorides have comparable solubility, silver iodide is appreciably less soluble than potassium iodide. The entropy changes for solution of the two sets of halides are comparable, but the heats of solution of the silver halides (other than the fluoride) are much greater (more positive) than those of the potassium salts. This is a consequence of the greater polarizing power of the silver ion in association with a large polarizable anion such as iodide, and the result is a reduction in solubility. When a silver halide dissolves in liquid ammonia, the solvent molecules are more polarizable than those of water, and consequently solubility is greater than in water. The polarizing power is greater for the B subgroup elements than for the corresponding A subgroup, with a progressive change occurring through a transition series. Thus the order of solubilities of the metal fluorides is $CaF_2 < MnF_2 < ZnF_2$ but with the more polarizable iodide ion the order of solubilities is $CaI_2 > MnI_2 > ZnI_2$.

TABLE 4

Solubility and heat of solution of some metal halides

	Solubility (mol dm^{-3})	Heat of solution (kJ mol^{-1})
KF	17·5	$-17 \cdot 1$
AgF	14·0	$-18 \cdot 0$
CaF$_2$	2×10^{-4}	$+16 \cdot 7$
MnF$_2$	0·12	$-90 \cdot 4$
ZnF$_2$	0·15	$-74 \cdot 1$
KI	8·9	$21 \cdot 3$
AgI	$1 \cdot 2 \times 10^{-8}$	$111 \cdot 0$
CaI$_2$	42	$-116 \cdot 0$
MnI$_2$		$-86 \cdot 6$
ZnI$_2$	13·7	$-57 \cdot 3$

Solution of covalent molecules

The hydrogen halides in the anhydrous state are covalent molecules but in aqueous solution, with the exception of hydrogen fluoride, they are extensively dissociated into ions. For a covalent molecule such as hydrogen chloride the energy steps can be shown as:

$$HCl(g) \rightarrow H(g) + Cl(g) \qquad \Delta H_1 = D(H{-}Cl) = 427 \text{ kJ mol}^{-1}$$

$$H(g) \rightarrow H^+(g) + e^- \qquad \Delta H_2 = I_H \qquad = 1318 \text{ kJ mol}^{-1}$$

$$Cl(g) + e^- \rightarrow Cl^-(g) \qquad \Delta H_3 = A_{Cl} \qquad = -364 \text{ kJ mol}^{-1}$$

$$H^+(g) + H_2O \rightarrow H^+(aq) \qquad \Delta H_4 = H_{hydn} \qquad = -1091 \text{ kJ mol}^{-1}$$

$$Cl^-(g) + H_2O \rightarrow Cl^-(aq) \qquad \Delta H_5 = H_{hydn} \qquad = -377 \text{ kJ mol}^{-1}$$

The overall heat of solution is given by

$$\Delta H_{soln} = \Delta H_1 + \Delta H_2 + \Delta H_3 + \Delta H_4 + \Delta H_5$$
$$= 427 + 1318 - 364 - 1091 - 377 = -87 \text{ kJ mol}^{-1}$$

The favourable enthalpy change for the formation of ions in the solution is due to the large enthalpy of hydration of the hydrogen ion. The value is much greater than for other singly-charged ions because of the very small size of the proton.

These simple calculations agree qualitatively with the known behaviour of metal salts. Other calculations in which calculated parameters, e.g. solubility product, are compared with experimentally determined values, indicate that the simple electrostatic representation of the interaction between an ion and the solvent gives a reasonable model of the aquated ion. It is not surprising to find that, when the ions do not behave as rigid charged spheres, deviations from the simple picture occur.

PROBLEMS

2.1. Use the Born equation to calculate the hydration enthalpies of Ca^{2+} and Cd^{2+}, where the crystal radii are 0·099 nm and 0·097 nm respectively. Compare these values with the measured values of -1580 kJ mol^{-1} for Ca^{2+} and -1805 kJ mol^{-1} for Cd^{2+}.

2.2. Calculate the concentrations in mol dm^{-3} of saturated solutions of (a) iron(II) hydroxide, and (b) iron(III) hydroxide. $K_{sp}(Fe(OH)_2) = 1 \times 10^{-14} \text{ mol}^3 \text{ dm}^{-9}$; $K_{sp}(Fe(OH)_3) = 1 \times 10^{-38} \text{ mol}^4 \text{ dm}^{-12}$.

2.3. Given the following data for the alkali-metal halides, calculate the heat of solution of rubidium iodide.

	NaCl	NaI	RbCl	RbI
Lattice energy/(kJ mol^{-1})	769·0	685·5	672·0	608·0
Heat of solution/(kJ mol^{-1})	3·8	$-7\cdot5$	17·1	?

2.4. Explain why there is an increase in entropy when H^+ and Cl^- are formed from HCl in the gas phase, but an entropy decrease when these ions are formed in aqueous solution.

2.5. A saturated solution of silver chloride contains 1.93×10^{-3} g dm^{-3} at 298 K. What is the heat of solution of silver chloride? Refer to Table 3 for entropy data.

3. Equilibrium reactions in solution

THE model of a solvated ion considered so far has assumed that interaction between the ion and the solvent is limited to the arrangement of the solvent molecules around the ions. In fact the ions may participate in further reactions, and these can be divided into two broad categories: reaction between the ions and the solvent and the reaction between the ions.

Hydrolysis

A reaction may occur between the metal ion and a water molecule in the coordination sphere in which a proton is released and the solution becomes acidic. This reaction is called *hydrolysis*, and in general terms can be denoted

$$A(H_2O)_x^{n+} \rightleftharpoons A(H_2O)_{x-1}OH^{(n-1)+} + H^+(aq)$$

Hydrolysis is not necessarily confined to a single reaction step: it may lead to the replacement of more than one coordinated water molecule. The general representation for additional hydrolysis steps is

$$A(H_2O)_{x-1}OH^{(n-1)+} \rightleftharpoons A(H_2O)_{x-2}(OH)_2^{(n-2)+} + H^+(aq)$$

$$A(H_2O)_{x-2}(OH)_2^{(n-2)+} \rightleftharpoons A(H_2O)_{x-3}(OH)_3^{(n-3)+} + H^+(aq)$$

until the last coordinated water molecule is removed in the final step

$$A(H_2O)(OH)_{x-1}^{(n-x+1)+} \rightleftharpoons A(OH)_x^{(n-x)+} + H^+(aq),$$

assuming that there is no change in coordination number. Thus there will be a series of equilibria in the solution, and since each hydrolysis step involves only the transfer of a proton, the system of equilibria will be rapidly established; see p. 94.

The equilibria may be disrupted if an insoluble compound is produced at some stage in the hydrolysis process. This occurs most frequently at the stage when the number of hydroxo-groups present is equal to the charge on the metal ion, and the metal hydroxide is precipitated:

$$A(H_2O)_{(x+1-n)}(OH)_{n-1}^+ \rightarrow A(OH)_n + (x-n)H_2O + H^+(aq)$$

For a number of metal ions the precipitate may be better represented as a hydrated oxide. An example is the precipitation of Fe^{3+} in which the product of the reaction is $Fe_2O_3 \cdot H_2O$, with some $FeO(OH)$ also present. On occasions there will also be uncertainty as to the formula of the species in solution. For example, when an even number of hydroxo-groups are present an alternative form may be written for the species in solution,

$$A(H_2O)_{x-2}(OH)_2^{(n-2)+} \rightarrow AO(H_2O)_{x-1}^{(n-2)+}$$
$$A(H_2O)_{x-4}(OH)_4^{(n-4)+} \rightarrow AO_2(H_2O)_{x-2}^{(n-4)+}$$

For many metal ions no distinction can be made between the two possible species and they are considered to be equivalent.

In some cases there is evidence in favour of oxo-species. The exchange of the aqueous uranium(VI) ion with labelled water is a slow reaction, and corresponds to exchange of two oxygen atoms for each uranium ion. This is interpreted in terms of the presence of the species $[UO_2(H_2O)_4]^{2+}$ in solution, rather than $[U(H_2O)_2(OH)_4]^{2+}$. The presence of an oxo-species may also be considered more probable when it is known to exist in the solid state. The existence of the uranyl series of compounds based on the ion UO_2^{2+} is well-established, and the exchange data are consistent with this fact.

The hydrolysis reaction should occur most readily with metal ions which will strongly polarize the coordinated water molecules, and facilitate the release of the proton. The polarizing power of the cation increases with increasing charge and decreasing size of the cation, and also increases from the A–subgroup elements through the transition elements to the B–subgroup elements. This is reflected in the observed hydrolysis of the metal cations. For elements of group IA hydrolysis of the M^+ cations does not occur to any significant extent, and in group IIA hydrolysis of the M^{2+} cations is confined mainly to ions of small radius, particularly Be^{2+}. For the transition elements and B–subgroup elements appreciable hydrolysis of the M^{2+} cation may occur, as with Zn, Cd, and Hg. For a given element hydrolysis of the cation increases as the oxidation state increases, and for a given oxidation state a cation of an element in the first transition series is more readily hydrolysed than the corresponding members of the second and third series.

The position of equilibrium of the hydrolysis reaction will be displaced by changing the concentration of any of the species present. Addition of acid will therefore drive the equilibria towards the simple aquo form, so that acid solutions of metal ions are used when hydrolysed species must be avoided. Quite strong acidities may be required. For example zinc, cadmium, and mercury M^{2+} ions are hydrolysed to MOH^+ if the acid strength of the solution is less than 0·1 M. Conversely, the addition of a base will displace the equilibrium to the right. In a number of cases the addition of base leads to the formation of hydroxo complex ions as the major species present. This behaviour is found with a number of metal hydroxides which dissolve in excess alkali.

The hydrolysis reaction may also lead to the formation of polymeric species that contain O or OH bridging groups. These reactions may be represented in general terms as

$$2M(H_2O)_x^{n+} \rightleftharpoons [(H_2O)_{x-1}M(OH)M(H_2O)_{x-1}]^{(2n-1)+} + H^+(aq)$$

$$2M(H_2O)_x^{n+} \rightleftharpoons [(H_2O)_{x-1}M\cdot O\cdot M(H_2O)_{x-1}]^{(2n-2)+} + 2H^+(aq)$$

such *condensation reactions* are not necessarily limited to a single stage; loss of a proton from an aquo-group in a partially-condensed species could lead to further condensation. The formation of polymeric species will be favoured by a decrease in hydrogen-ion concentration and by an increase in metal-ion concentration. Insoluble oxides or hydroxides may be formed in the final stage of a polymerization reaction; such precipitates should therefore not be regarded as the simple species usually written in a stoicheiometric equation.

Metal hydroxides of low solubility have a solubility product $K_{sp} = a_{M^{n+}} \cdot a_{OH^-}^n$, and the maximum pH of the solution before precipitation occurs will depend on the concentration of the metal ion and the solubility product. The a_{OH^-} may be replaced by K_w/a_{H^+}, where K_w is the ionic product for water, and rewriting in logarithmic form,

$$pH = \frac{1}{n}\lg K_{sp} - \frac{1}{n}\lg a_{M^{n+}} - \lg K_w$$

The solubility product decreases with increasing charge on the cation, so that, for a given metal-ion concentration, precipitation occurs at lower pH the higher the charge on the cation, as shown in Table 5.

TABLE 5

Solubility product and pH of precipitation of metal ions $(0.01 \text{ mol dm}^{-3})$
as hydroxides

	$K_{sp}/(\text{mol}^3 \text{ dm}^{-9})$	$K_{sp}/(\text{mol}^4 \text{ dm}^{-12})$	$K_{sp}/(\text{mol}^5 \text{ dm}^{-15})$	pH of precipitation
Mg^{2+}	1.3×10^{-10}			10.0
Ca^{2+}	1×10^{-17}			6.5
Fe^{2+}	1×10^{-14}			8.0
Cu^{2+}	5.0×10^{-19}			5.5
Al^{3+}		3.7×10^{-15}		9.8
Cr^{3+}		6.7×10^{-31}		4.8
Fe^{3+}		1×10^{-38}		2.1
Ti^{4+}			7.9×10^{-54}	1.2

Complex-ion formation

The second category of reactions of the aquated ions covers the reaction between ions of opposite charge, and leads to replacement of water molecules in the coordination sphere. The replacement reactions can be represented by a series of equilibria in which one water molecule is replaced by an ionic species in each step.

$$A(H_2O)_x^{n+} + X^- \rightleftharpoons A(H_2O)_{x-1}X^{(n-1)+} + H_2O \qquad K_1$$

$$A(H_2O)_{x-1}X^{(n-1)+} + X^- \rightleftharpoons A(H_2O)_{x-2}X^{(n-2)+} + H_2O \qquad K_2$$

$$A(H_2O)X_{x-1}^{(n-x+1)+} + X^- \rightleftharpoons AX_x^{(n-x)+} + H_2O \qquad K_x$$

Each step will be an equilibrium process with an equilibrium constant K_n. Since they represent the addition of one anion at a time the equilibrium constants are called step-wise formation constants, with reference to the formation of the complex ion on the right-hand side of the equation. The formation constant K_1 will be of the form

$$K_1 = \frac{a_{AX^{(n-1)+}}}{a_{A^{n+}} \cdot a_{X^-}}$$

where the number of water molecules in the hydration sphere has been omitted. It must be remembered that the tabulated values of the step-wise formation constants, although written in this way, refer to an association between the anion and the hydrated cations. The size of the step-wise formation constants is a measure of the amount of a given complex species present in the solution. This will obviously depend upon the properties of the metal ion and the ligand.

For a number of metal ions the size of the formation constant for reaction with a given ligand can be explained in terms of an electrostatic model, K increases with increasing charge and decreasing size of the cation. Similarly, for a given cation the smaller F^- ion produces a more stable complex than the larger Cl^- ion: $K_{FeF^{2+}} = 1 \times 10^6$ mol^{-1} dm^3, $K_{FeCl^{2+}} = 2 \times 10^1$ mol^{-1} dm^3. It is also worthy of note that the large ion ClO_4^- has very little tendency to form complex ions. Hence perchloric acid is frequently used to prevent hydrolysis of metal ions, because it avoids the added problem of the formation of complexes between the metal ion and the anion of the acid. However, for other metal ions additional factors become increasingly important and may lead to a reversed order of stability; thus for the Hg^{2+} ion, $K_{HgF^+} = 4 \times 10^1$ mol^{-1} dm^3 and $K_{HgCl^+} = 5 \times 10^6$ mol^{-1} dm^3. No simple interpretation of the trends in formation constants can be given, because the observed free-energy change is again a small difference between large terms. Changes in factors which have relatively minor effects on the free energies of the product or the reactants can have a very significant effect on the formation constant. Thus a difference of 8 kJ mol^{-1} in the free-energy change in a reaction will alter the formation constant by a factor of about 30.

The species present in solution when a metal salt is dissolved will depend not only on the nature of the cation but also on the nature of the anion which is inevitably present, and solutions of simple salts may contain complex ions.

Complex species may also be formed by the addition of solutions containing other molecules or ions. For example basic solutions of Ni^{2+} or Fe^{3+} salts are readily hydrolysed to the insoluble hydroxides. The hydroxides show little tendency to react further with base to give soluble oxo- or hydroxo-complexes. The addition of aqueous ammonia to the suspension will dissolve the nickel hydroxide but not the iron(III) hydroxide. This is a result of the establishment of a further set of equilibria in the solution,

$$M(NH_3)_x^{n+} \rightleftharpoons M(H_2O)_{x-1}NH_3^{n+} \overset{NH_3}{\rightleftharpoons} M(H_2O)_x^{n+} \rightleftharpoons M(H_2O)_{x-1}OH^{(n-1)+}$$
$$\rightleftharpoons M(OH)_n$$

The steps leading to formation of the precipitate lie to the right of the equation and the steps leading to the formation of soluble ammine complexes lie to the left. The size of the step-wise formation constants for the reaction between nickel(II) and ammonia indicate that the equilibrium will lie well to the left, but probably not as far as the addition of six ammonia molecules. The concentration of the simple aquo-species is reduced considerably so that even if the equilibria involving the hydroxo-species are present to any extent, the concentrations involved do not exceed the solubility product of nickel hydroxide. On the other hand iron(III) has a very low affinity for ammonia, so that the equilibrium is maintained well to the right and the 'hydroxide' remains insoluble.

The interaction between the ions may be of a form in which the coordinated water is not replaced, and instead the anion is separated from the metal ion by the coordination sphere of water molecules. Ion association of this type is described as an outer-sphere complex as opposed to the coordination complexes already discussed. Outer-sphere complexes are most easily studied when the formation of coordination complexes is a slow process, as with cobalt(III) complex ions. The interaction between $Co(NH_3)_5H_2O^{3+}$ and the SO_4^{2-} ions has been interpreted in terms of an outer-sphere complex with a formation constant of $2 \times 10^3 \ mol^{-1} \ dm^3$. The enthalpy of interaction is very small, as might be expected with a sphere of water molecules separating the charged species, and the main driving force for the reaction is a large favourable entropy change arising from the release of water molecules from the solvation sphere. The effect of a decrease in relative permittivity has already been noted, where this leads to increased ion association and changes in the observed properties of the solution (p. 6).

Electrode potentials†

A metal ion in solution may be reduced to a lower oxidation state or oxidized to a higher oxidation state. The ease with which these reactions may

† A full account of electrode potentials is given by J. Robbins in *Ions in solution* (2): *an introduction to electrochemistry* (OCS 2).

occur can be shown in terms of the general equilibrium,

$$M^{a+} + (a-b)e^- \rightleftharpoons M^{b+} \qquad \text{where } 0 \leqslant b < a$$

For a reduction there will be a net loss of hydration energy, since the hydration energy decreases with decreasing charge and increasing size, but the addition of an electron to a cation is an energetically favourable process. The balance between these two energy terms controls the equilibrium position. When metal atoms are produced the hydration-energy term is replaced by the heat of atomization.

The electrode potential of a solution containing the ions M^{a+} and M^{b+} is given by the Nernst equation

$$E = E^{\ominus} + \frac{RT}{nF} \ln \{a_{M^{a+}}/a_{M^{b+}}\}$$

where
n = the number of electrons transferred per ion (a − b)
F = the Faraday = 9.649×10^4 C mol^{-1}
R = the gas constant = 8.314 J K^{-1} mol^{-1}
T = the thermodynamic temperature
$a_{M^{a+}}$ = the activity of M^{a+} ions in the solution
$a_{M^{b+}}$ = the activity of M^{b+} ions in solution
E = the electrode potential of the solution
$E^{\ominus}$ = the standard electrode potential

Any species added to the solution which reduces the activity of either M^{a+} or M^{b+} and alters the ratio $a_{M^{a+}}/a_{M^{b+}}$ will change the observed potential. The standard electrode potential $E^{\ominus}$ is the potential of the solution when the ions are in their standard states, viz. at unit activity, and the values of $E^{\ominus}$ are tabulated.‡ The free-energy change, electrode potential, and equilibrium constant for a given reaction are related by

$$\Delta G^{\ominus} = -nFE^{\ominus} = -RT \ln K$$

where the superscript $\ominus$ specifies standard states of reactants and products.

Since the free-energy change for an oxidation or reduction may be calculated from the electrode potential it follows that the possible oxidation or reduction of one ion by another may be calculated in this way. The rule to remember is that where the electrode potential of $M^{n+}/M^{(n-1)+}$ is larger (more positive) than the electrode potential of $A^{a+}/A^{(a-1)+}$ the M^{n+} will be reduced by $A^{(a-1)+}$. For the consecutive reduction

$$M^{2+} + e^- \rightarrow M^+ \qquad M^+ + e^- \rightarrow M$$

if the electrode potential of the first step is less than the electrode potential for the second step then M^+ will be unstable with respect to the disproportionation reaction $2M^+ \rightarrow M + M^{2+}$.

‡ See Robbins (1972) p. 62.

The electrode potential not only provides information about the position of equilibrium between different oxidation states, but also a measure of the stability of the ions in solution. The electrode potential is therefore useful in the discussion of disproportionation and the possible use of an ion as an oxidizing or reducing species.

PROBLEMS

3.1. The solubility product of silver bromide is $7.7 \times 10^{-13} \ mol^2 \ dm^{-6}$. What is the solubility of silver bromide? What is the solubility of silver bromide when ammonia is added to the suspension, if the ammonia concentration is maintained at $0.4 \ mol \ dm^{-3}$? The stability constant of $Ag(NH_3)_2^+$ is $1.6 \times 10^7 \ mol^{-2} \ dm^6$.

3.2. You are given the following electrode potentials: $Cu^+/Cu \quad E^\ominus = 0.52 \ V$, $Cu^{2+}/Cu^+ \quad E^\ominus = 0.153 \ V$, $Cu^{2+}/CuCl \quad E^\ominus = 0.54 \ V$, $CuCl/Cu \quad E^\ominus = 0.14 \ V$. (a) Calculate the equilibrium constant for the reaction $2Cu^+ \rightleftharpoons Cu + Cu^{2+}$ at 298 K. (b) Will copper(I) disproportionate in aqueous solution? (c) What effect will added chloride ions have on the disproportionation reaction?

3.3. The solubility of silver chloride in aqueous solution is reduced by the addition of sodium chloride but the solubility of copper(I) chloride is increased. Explain these observations.

3.4. From the following electrode potentials calculate the solubility product of silver iodide at 298 K: $E^\ominus_{AgI,Ag} = -0.15 \ V$, $E^\ominus_{Ag^+,Ag} = 0.80 \ V$.

3.5. The step-wise hydrolysis constants of $Hg^{2+}(aq)$ are $K_1 = 10^{-3.7} \ mol \ dm^{-3}$ and $K_2 = 10^{-2.6} \ mol \ dm^{-3}$. (a) If the solution is maintained at pH = 3 calculate the proportion of the total mercury present as Hg^{2+}, $HgOH^+$, and $Hg(OH)_2$. (b) If the solution is then acidified to pH = 1 calculate the proportion of the total mercury present as Hg^{2+}.

4. Acids and bases

A DISCUSSION of acids and bases must begin with a definition of the two terms, and of the various definitions put forward that of Brønsted and Lowry is appropriate here. An *acid* is defined as a molecule or ion which has a tendency to transfer a proton to another molecule or ion in a chemical reaction, while a *base* is defined as a molecule or ion which has a tendency to gain a proton. With this definition the general reaction of an acid with a base is

$$HA + B^- \rightarrow A^- + BH$$

A commonly-encountered acid–base reaction is the reaction between hydrogen chloride and sodium hydroxide in aqueous solution. If the ionization of the two compounds in aqueous solution is taken into account then the overall neutralization reaction is

$$H^+ + OH^- \rightarrow H_2O$$

so that in aqueous solution an acid is a compound which transfers a proton to water and a base is a compound which accepts a proton from water. The two general reactions would be

$$HA + H_2O \rightleftharpoons H_3O^+ + A^-$$

$$B^- + H_2O \rightleftharpoons HB + OH^-$$

These are yet further examples of the equilibria which can be established in aqueous solution. In the first equilibrium H_3O^+ and HA behave as acids, while H_2O and A^- act as bases. In the second equilibrium H_2O and HB are acids while B^- and OH^- act as bases. The acid HA and the base A^- which differ only by H^+ are known as a *conjugate pair*. Acids and bases which are extensively ionized in dilute solutions are described as 'strong'; acids and bases which are not extensively ionized are described as 'weak'.

Pure water dissociates into the ions H^+ and OH^-, a process known as auto-ionization, and the extent of the ionization is given by the ionic product $K_w = a_{H^+}a_{OH^-} = 10^{-14}$ mol^2 dm^{-6} at 25°C. For a neutral solution $a_{H^+} = a_{OH^-} = 10^{-7}$ mol dm^{-3}. Aqueous solutions with $a_{H^+} > 10^{-7}$ are acidic; when $a_{OH^-} > 10^{-7}$ the solutions are basic. However since the product $a_{H^+}a_{OH^-}$ is a constant a basic solution will still contain hydrogen ions and an acid solution will still contain hydroxide ions. The a_{H^+} is usually quoted in terms of the pH of the solution, where pH $= -\lg a_{H^+}$; when $a_{H^+} = 10^{-2}$ the pH $= 2$.

The acidity of a given solute in aqueous solution will be the net result of two competing equilibrium reactions. The acid dissociation of the solute will be represented by

$$HA + H_2O \rightleftharpoons H_3O^+ + A^- \qquad \text{with free-energy change } \Delta G_1$$

and the acid dissociation of the solvent by

$$H_2O + H_2O \rightleftharpoons H_3O^+ + OH^- \qquad \text{with free-energy change } \Delta G_2$$

Combination of these two equations gives

$$HA + OH^- \rightleftharpoons H_2O + A^- \qquad \text{with free-energy change } \Delta G = \Delta G_1 - \Delta G_2$$

which is identical with the general equation written for an acid–base reaction. For this equilibrium to lie to the right (with HA behaving as an acid) requires $\Delta G_1 < \Delta G_2$. Since $\Delta G^\ominus = -RT \ln K$ and for the acid dissociation of water $K = 10^{-16}$ it follows that K for the solute must be greater than 10^{-16} if the solute is to be an acid in aqueous solution. Thus ethanol will not be considered an acid in aqueous solution, since the acid dissociation constant is 10^{-18}, but phosphoric acid H_3PO_4 will ionize with the liberation of hydrogen ions, because the dissociation constants for the three steps are $K_1 = 9 \times 10^{-3}$, $K_2 = 6 \times 10^{-8}$, and $K_3 = 1 \times 10^{-12}$. When the solvent is changed lower values of the acid dissociation constant for the solvent correspond to increased (more positive) values of ΔG_2. Increased acid dissociation of the solvent leads to lower values of ΔG_2. Consequently the extent of ionization of HA will depend on the acid dissociation constant of the solvent.

The acid HA and the base A^- form a conjugate pair, and if HA is a strong acid then A^- is a weak base. The converse is also true. The ion A^- is a base in water as a result of the hydrolysis reaction

$$A^- + H_2O \rightleftharpoons HA + OH^-$$

Thus a salt of a weak acid in aqueous solution will dissociate and undergo hydrolysis to form the weak acid (undissociated) and hydroxide ions, and so make the solution basic.

The strength of an acid is described in terms of the acid dissociation constant K_a, which is an equilibrium constant for the reaction $HA + H_2O \rightleftharpoons H_3O^+ + A^-$, such that $K_a = a_{H_3O^+} a_{A^-} / a_{HA}$. This expression may be expressed in terms of concentrations for very dilute solutions, when concentrations are equal to activities, and the activity of water is unity. Although only approximately true at higher concentrations the expression $K_a \sim c_{H_3O^+} c_{A^-} / c_{HA}$ will provide a measure of the strength of an acid. A similar definition applies to a base, where the equilibrium constant refers to the reaction $B^- + H_2O \rightleftharpoons HB + OH^-$ and $K_b = a_{HB} a_{OH^-} / a_{B^-}$. Alternatively the reaction may be written as $B^- + H_3O^+ \rightleftharpoons HB + H_2O$ with an equilibrium constant $K = a_{HB} / a_{B^-} a_{H_3O^+} = K_b / a_{H_3O^+} a_{OH^-} = K_b / K_w$ where K_w is the *ionic product of water*.

Base strength may be given in terms of either of the equilibrium constants K or K_b, which differ only by $K_w = 10^{-14}$. The acid strength is frequently expressed in terms of pK_a which is equal to $-\lg K_a$; e.g., when $K_a = 10^{-3}$, $pK_a = 3$.

In a strongly basic solvent, proton transfer from the acid to the solvent occurs more readily and many acids will then be 'strong'

$$HA + HB \rightleftharpoons A^- + H_2B^+$$
acid base base acid
(solvent)

The acidity of every strong acid is 'levelled' to the strength of the ion H_2B^+, which is the strongest acid that can exist in a protonated solvent. This means that the strongest acid which can exist in a protonated solvent is the acid produced by auto-ionization of the solvent,

$$2HB \rightleftharpoons B^- + H_2B^+$$

Acetic acid is as strong as nitric acid or perchloric acid in liquid ammonia, but in a less basic solvent such as water, acetic acid is weak, while nitric acid and perchloric acid remain strong. When the concentration of H_2B^+ ions becomes proportional to the strength of the acid, the acids are said to be 'differentiated' according to their proton donor properties.

When a base is added to a solvent, proton transfer from the solvent to the base occurs

$$B^- + HA \rightleftharpoons HB + A^-$$

A decrease in acid character of the solvent produces a change from complete protonation of the base in acetic acid to a lower degree of protonation of the base in water. In acetic acid bases will be 'levelled' to the basicity of the acetate ion, while in water they may be 'differentiated' according to their proton acceptor properties. However very strong bases such as ethoxide $C_2H_5O^-$ or amide NH_2^- will still be completely protonated in water and the base strength levelled to that of the hydroxide ion

$$B^- + H_2O \rightleftharpoons HB + OH^-.$$

Buffer solutions

Although a solution of a weak acid HA is almost entirely undissociated the sodium salt of the acid NaA, is extensively dissociated in solution. If the expression for K_a is rewritten as $c_{H_3O^+} \sim K_a c_{HA}/c_{A^-}$ then it follows that the hydrogen-ion concentration in the solution containing a mixture of a weak acid and its salt depends only on K_a and the ratio c_{HA}/c_{A^-}. For a weak acid c_{HA} is virtually the total acid concentration and for a strong electrolyte c_{A^-} is approximately the total salt concentration. The solution may be diluted without change of c_{H^+}, but more importantly the solutions remain at the same pH when small amounts of strong acid or base are added. Because of this property of maintaining a constant pH, solutions containing a mixture of weak acids and their salts or a mixture of weak bases and their salts are called *buffer solutions*. In the above example protons combine with A^- to form undissociated HA, while excess base combines with HA to form A^- ions. If 10^{-3} mol of hydrochloric acid is added to 1 dm^3 (a litre) of pure water the hydrogen-ion concentration changes by a factor of 10^4. Consider the effect of adding the same quantity of hydrochloric acid to 1 dm^3 of solution containing 0·5 mol of acetic acid and 0·5 mol of sodium acetate. K_a for acetic acid is $1·85 \times 10^{-5}$ mol dm^{-3}. The hydrogen-ion concentration of the buffer solution $= (0·5/0·5) \times 1·8 \times 10^{-5}$ mol dm^{-3}. When 10^{-3} mol of hydrochloric acid is added the protons combine with acetate ions to form undissociated acetic acid. The concentration c_{HA} is now 0·501 mol dm^{-3}, and the concentration of A^- is now equal to 0·499 mol dm^{-3}. The hydrogen-ion concentration is now $(0·501/0·499) \times 1·85 \times 10^{-5}$ mol dm^{-3}, changing only by the factor $(0·501/0·499)$, and is essentially unchanged.

Complex cations as acids

Certain hydrated cations are hydrolysed with the liberation of protons, producing acid solutions. Consequently the factors which lead to hydrolysis of the cation will also lead to the cations behaving as acids (see p. 21).

TABLE 6

Acid dissociation constants of some complex ions

Ion	pK_1	pK_2
$Co(NH_3)_6^{3+}$	>14	
$Co(NH_3)_5H_2O^{3+}$	6·6	
$Rh(NH_3)_6^{3+}$	>14	
$Rh(NH_3)_5H_2O^{3+}$	5·9	
$Pt(NH_3)_6^{4+}$	7·2	10·5
$Pt(NH_3)_5Cl^{3+}$	8·4	
$Pt(NH_3)_5H_2O^{4+}$	4·0	
cis-$Coen_2(H_2O)_2^{3+}$	6·1	8·2

Complex cations other than simple aquo ions may also function as acids. If the complex ion still contains coordinated water, $M(H_2O)_xA_y$, then dissociation of a water molecule may occur. Results for a limited number of complexes show a comparable acidity for the complexes $[M(H_2O)_xA_y]^{n+}$ and $[M(H_2O)_x(OH)_y]^{n+}$. Complexes containing ammine ligands are frequently acids of measurable strength (Table 6). A knowledge of these dissociation constants is important since they govern the behaviour of the complexes at different pH. Ammine complexes are generally less acidic than aquo complexes, which is in qualitative agreement with the lower acidity of the ammonium ion NH_4^+ compared with the hydronium ion H_3O^+. Complexes may also function as acids by the formation of outer-sphere complexes between an inert complex ion and a hydroxide ion.

Acidic and basic oxides

The reaction between an oxide and water may produce an acidic or a basic solution depending on the element with which the oxygen is combined. At one extreme there are the oxides of the group IA and IIA elements which dissolve to form strongly basic solutions. The ionic lattice of the solute dissociates in the solvent to produce the hydrated cation and the oxide ion. The latter can be considered as a powerful base which is levelled to the strength of the hydroxide ion.

$$M_2O + H_2O \rightarrow 2M^+(aq) + 2OH^-(aq)$$

The association of the aquated ions increases with decreasing size of the cation. Thus in group IA LiOH is the weakest base. The increased charge on the group IIA cations leads to increased association of the cations and anions. The extent of ion association is greater in the corresponding B subgroups, but in group IB the hydroxides are unstable and decompose to the hydrated oxide. The increasing ion association in group IIB differs from ion association in group IIA in that it increases with increasing size of the cation (Table 7), indicating again the importance of polarization with the B-subgroup elements.

TABLE 7

Stability constants for the formation of $M(OH)(aq)$ and $M(OH)^+(aq)$

	$\lg K_1$		$\lg K_1$
Li^+	0·2	Mg^{2+}	2·57
Na^+	−0·6	Ca^{2+}	1·5
K^+	†	Sr^{2+}	0·9
Rb^+	†	Ba^{2+}	0·7
		Zn^{2+}	4·4
		Cd^{2+}	4·5
		Hg^{2+}	11·5

† No evidence of complex formation.

The most comprehensive reference for stability constants of all the elements is L. G. Sillen and A. E. Martell, *Stability constants of metal-ion complexes*, and Supplement No. 1. Special Publications Nos. 17 and 25. The Chemical Society, London.

The other extreme for the reactions between an oxide and water is shown by the covalent oxides of groups VIB and VIIB. These oxides abstract hydroxyl groups from the solvent, releasing protons in the process:

$$XO_3 + H_2O \rightarrow XO_2(OH)_2 \rightarrow XO_3(OH)^- + H^+(aq).$$

The solution of these oxides in water produces oxo-acids, and the acidity arises from the ionization of the hydroxyl groups attached to the central atom X. The acidity of the oxo-acids shows a strong dependence on the number of oxygen atoms. For oxo-acids of general formula $(HO)_a XO_b$ the acidity is often independent of the central atom X and the ratio of the successive acid dissociation constants is

$$K_1/K_2 \sim K_2/K_3 \sim 10^5$$

The behaviour described for the reaction between oxides and water does not take into account the polymerization of acidic and basic oxo-compounds which may take place in solution; only the strong bases of group IA and the strong acids of group VIIB do not polymerize. The basicity of the oxides generally increases down a group. Consequently weak bases are formed by the lighter members of a group—beryllium in group IIA—and weak acids are formed by the heavier members of a group—tellurium in group VIB. It is these weak acids and bases which show the greatest tendency to polymerize.

There is no simple correlation between the polymeric species present and pH, with no evidence for a regular increase in polymerization, monomer → dimer → trimer → n-mer, with increasing pH. The main polymeric species present in the hydrolysis of $Be^{2+}(aq)$ is $Be_3(OH)_3^{3+}$, while in $Cu^{2+}(aq)$ hydrolysis the main species present is $Cu_2(OH)_2^{2+}$ with a small amount of $CuOH^+$. The formation of the insoluble hydroxide precipitates may be considered as the last stage in the polymerization process.

Polyanions

The reaction leading to the formation of polyanions may be written in general terms as

$$MO_4^{n-} + MO_4^{n-} = M_2O_7^{(2n-2)-} + O^{2-}$$

$$O^{2-} + 2H^+ = H_2O$$

Polymerization should occur most readily with anions having the greatest tendency to lose oxide ions, and this tendency will be greater with increasing negative charge on the oxygen in the M—O bond. This will occur as the electronegativity of M decreases, and it is the elements of low electronegativity that form the weak oxo-acids. The two reactions written for the polymerization suggest that it should be favoured in acid solution. The anions are linked through common oxygen atoms into polymers which may be either rings or chains. The condensation may be brought about by changing the pH of the solution or by increasing the concentration of the monomeric anion.

Amphoteric oxides

Some oxides may function as either acids or bases, depending upon the pH of the solution: these are the *amphoteric oxides*. The series of equilibria which are established for amphoteric species have already been described (p. 20), so only the extreme cases of acid reaction and basic reaction will be given here. The acid function may be shown by the equilibrium

$$Al_2O_3 + 9H_2O \rightleftharpoons 2Al(OH)_6^{3-} + 6H^+$$

and the basic function by the equilibrium

$$Al_2O_3 + 3H_2O \rightleftharpoons 2Al^{3+}(aq) + 6OH^-$$

The amphoteric behaviour will be more readily exhibited if base is added in the first reaction to remove the protons and if acid is added in the second reaction to remove the hydroxide ions. No simple explanation of amphoteric behaviour can be given, but in general the elements which form amphoteric oxides are (a) the elements near the boundary between the metals and the non-metals in the periodic table and (b) the transition elements.

Examination of the equilibrium reactions for acidic and basic behaviour of a metal oxide show that qualitatively at least (a) is to be expected. If the

$$H^+ + MO^- \rightleftharpoons MOH \rightleftharpoons M^+ + OH^-$$

polarization of the M—OH bond is high the bond will have considerable covalent character, and in the limit approaches the bonding in a non-metal oxide, which leads to entirely acid behaviour. If there is very little polarization of the M—OH bond, the bond will be essentially ionic, and this produces only basic behaviour. Thus, for the oxide to exhibit amphoteric properties the extent of polarization must be carefully balanced, and is most likely to occur with elements on the boundary of the metals and non-metals. For the transition elements amphoteric behaviour is found more frequently with the elements in higher oxidation states, which is consistent with a dependence on polarization of the M—OH bond. The amphoteric non-transition elements are shown in Table 8.

TABLE 8

Non-transition elements that form ampho-teric oxides

Be					
	Al				
	Sc	Zn	Ga		
				Sn	Sb
				Pb	

In the first transition series amphoteric behaviour is found for cations of decreasing oxidation state moving to the right across the period. Thus Ti^{4+}, V^{4+}, Co^{3+}, Cu^{2+}, and Zn^{2+} are amphoteric species illustrating this trend. Elements in the second and third series show a reduction in acidity: ions in the corresponding oxidation states are larger, and so amphoteric behaviour occurs with ions in higher oxidation states, but still decreasing across the series. The behaviour of the transition-metal oxides fits into the general pattern of behaviour for acidic and basic oxides. The higher oxides are more covalent and hence acidic, while the lower oxides are more ionic and hence basic in character.

Polarization effects

Reference has been made in the preceding discussion to polarizing interaction between ions and to changes in this effect across the periodic table. When a cation and an anion approach one another the field around each ion polarizes the other ion, the major effect usually being the polarization of the anion by the cation. The ultimate result of this polarizing effect is the transfer of electrons from one ion to the other, giving a covalent bond.

The polarizing power of a cation increases with increasing charge and decreasing size, while the polarizability of the anion increases with increasing charge and increasing size, and decreases with increasing electronegativity. For a large polarizable anion the polarizing effect is greater with cations exhibiting group valence moving from left to right in the periodic table. Additional effects will be found where the effective nuclear charge of the cation differs from the formal nuclear charge. The increasing nuclear charge across the long periods (particularly in the third long period with the lanthanides and third transition series elements) leads to a general increase in ionization potential for the formation of the divalent ion, and conversely to an increased electron affinity of the divalent ion. This arises because the form of the radial distribution function of an ns orbital results in the ns electron experiencing a pronounced increased effective nuclear charge when it penetrates inside the underlying filled or partly filled $(n-1)d$ and $(n-2)f$ shells (Fig. 5).

The observed changes in covalent character within the periodic table can be rationalized in these terms,† and an attempt has been made to explain the observed behaviour in terms of 'hard' and 'soft' acids and bases. 'Hard' acids are cations of small size and high charge with no π-bonding electrons. 'Soft' acids have the opposite properties. 'Hard' bases are anions of small size, low charge, and with filled π-orbitals. 'Soft' bases have opposite properties in these respects.

Reactions are then interpreted in terms of a generalized acid–base definition, in which an acid is defined as a species which has a tendency to accept electrons while a base has a tendency to donate electrons. (Acids and bases defined in this way are sometimes called Lewis acids and Lewis bases.) This

† For more details see R. J. Puddephatt's *The periodic table of the elements* (OCS 3).

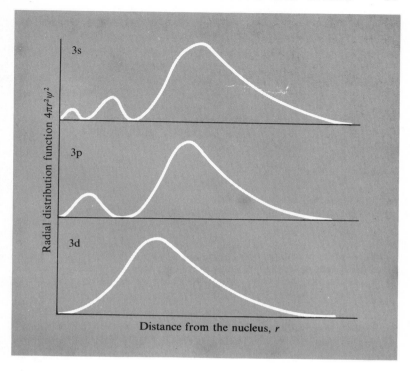

3s

3p

3d

Radial distribution function $4\pi r^2 \psi^2$

Distance from the nucleus, r

FIG. 5. Plot of radial distribution function $4\pi r^2 \psi^2$ against distance from the nucleus.

TABLE 9

Hard and soft acids and bases

	Acids	Bases
Hard	H^+, Li^+, Na^+, K^+ $Be^{2+}, Mg^{2+}, Ca^{2+}, Mn^{2+}, UO_2^{2+}$ $Si^{4+}, Ti^{4+}, Zr^{4+}$	H_2O, OH^-, F^-, Cl^- ClO_4^-, NO_3^- NH_3, RNH_2
Soft	Cu^+, Ag^+, Tl^+, Hg^+ $Pd^{2+}, Cd^{2+}, Pt^{2+}$ Pt^{4+}, Te^{4+}	RS^-, I^-, SCN^- R_3P, CN^-, CO H^-

covers a very wide range of reactions which can be written generally as $A + :B \rightarrow A:B$. The general principle covering these reactions is that hard acids prefer to coordinate with hard bases, while soft acids prefer to co-ordinate with soft bases. The variations in the solubilities of the Ag^+ halides compared with the K^+ halides, and the varying acidities of hydroxides, are interpreted in terms of variations in the covalency of the bonds involved. Polarization of the ions produces deviations from the pattern of behaviour expected on a simple electrostatic model, so that any summary of the trends in these effects within the periodic table will be useful. The idea of hard and soft acids and bases is one such generalization.

PROBLEMS

4.1. Will the following compounds form acidic, basic, or neutral aqueous solutions? Explain your answers. (a) Sodium acetate (b) Sodium chloride (c) Ammonium chloride (d) Iron(II) chloride (e) Iron(III) chloride.

4.2. An aqueous solution containing 0.01 mol dm^{-3} of potassium cyanide has pH $= 10.6$. Calculate K_a for hydrocyanic acid.

4.3. Calculate the pH of the following aqueous solutions: (a) 1M acetic acid (b) 1M acetic acid and 1M sodium acetate, and (c) 1M acetic acid and 0.1M sodium acetate. K_a for acetic acid is 1.8×10^{-5} mol dm^{-3}.

4.4. What are the conjugate acids of O^{2-}, NH_3, CO_3^{2-}, and $Al(H_2O)_5OH^{2+}$? What are the conjugate bases of H_2CO_3, H_2O, HSO_4^-, and $Co(NH_3)_6^{3+}$?

4.5. Pyridine is a weak base in water. If you wanted to titrate it as a strong base would you use acetic acid or liquid ammonia as solvent? Explain your choice.

5. The elements of group IA and group IIA

Group IA

Solubility

THE salts of the group IA elements are soluble as a general rule, and produce aquo-ions with a probable coordination number of four for Li, Na, and K, and a probable coordination number of six for Cs. Lithium salts are frequently less soluble in water than the corresponding salts of the other alkali metals (p. 6). The fact that lithium salts are soluble at all is a result of the large enthalpy of hydration of the small lithium cation. The interaction with water is such that there is an overall increase in structure in the solution and the cation has a negative entropy of solution. The larger cations of K, Rb, and Cs disrupt the water structure and have positive entropies of solution which favour the solution process and compensate for the less favourable enthalpies

TABLE 10

Some properties of the group IA metals

	Li	Na	K	Rb	Cs
Ionic radius/nm	0·060	0·095	0·133	0·147	0·174
Ionization potentials/(kJ mol^{-1})					
First	517·1	493·9	416·8	401·4	373·4
Second	7263·0	4540·0	3054·0		
Standard electrode potential/V	−3·02	−2·71	−2·92	−2·99	−3·02
Enthalpy of hydration/(kJ mol^{-1})	514·6	405·8	322·1	292·8	263·6

of solution. In general the small cations form their least soluble salts with small cations, while the large cations form their least soluble salts with large anions. The oxides and hydroxides dissolve readily to give strongly basic solutions. There are few precipitation reactions of the group IA cations and these are confined almost entirely to salts containing a large cation and a large anion. The perchlorates, ClO_4^-, of potassium, rubidium, and caesium have low solubility, as do the hexanitrocobaltates, $[Co(NO_2)_6]^{3-}$; the tetraphenylborates, $(C_6H_5)_4B^-$, can be precipitated quantitatively from aqueous solution. Double salts such as alums can be crystallized out when concentrated solutions of the two sulphates are mixed, probably because a large ion of low charge is formed. Reference has already been made to the evidence for the formation of outer-sphere complexes containing the sulphate anion, (p. 24), and in a nearly saturated solution outer-sphere complexes may be produced in appreciable concentration. The result of this complex formation is that a large anion of low charge is produced from two smaller ions with a higher ratio of charge to radius:

$$Al(H_2O)_6^{3+} + 2SO_4^{2-}(aq) \rightarrow [Al(H_2O)_6^{3+} \cdot (SO_4^{2-})_2]^-$$

The solubility of such an anion combined with a moderately large univalent cation would be low.

Where polarization of the anion can occur then the amount of polarization increases with decreasing size of the cation. In non-polar solvents the effect of polarization may be great enough for ion pairs to be formed. These increase the stability of the species in solution and therefore increase the solubility of the salt. Thus sodium iodide is soluble in acetone (~ 3 M at 25°C) but potassium iodide has little solubility (~ 0.01 M at 25°C). The high solubility of lithium and sodium perchlorates in oxygenated non-aqueous solvents is unlikely to arise in this way because of the very low polarizability of the perchlorate anion. It is suggested that with an oxo-solvent the solvation enthalpy of the small cations may still be sufficiently large to favour the solution against the crystal lattice.

The alkali metals dissolve in liquid ammonia, the stability of the solution decreasing with increasing size of the metal atom. The solutions have a characteristic blue colour which is ascribed to the presence of solvated electrons. The general solution reaction can be shown as

$$M \rightleftharpoons M_{solv}^+ + e_{solv}^-.$$

The cations so formed are apparently identical in properties with the cations obtained by solution of a salt MA. The solutions have powerful reducing properties, but since these are independent of the cation present, the nature of the solvated electron will be considered at a later stage (p. 86).

Hydrolysis

The hydrated cations of group IA show little tendency to hydrolyse.

$$M(H_2O)_x^+ \rightarrow M(H_2O)_{x-1}OH + H^+$$

Consequently, although the solutions of salts may contain different hydrated forms in equilibrium, change of pH will have no significant effect on the species present.

Complex ions

The alkali-metal cations show little tendency to form complex ions with a wide range of ligands in aqueous solution. A series of complexes is formed, however, with cyclic polyethers of the type

The complex produced depends on the number of oxygen atoms in the cyclic polyether. In complexes with 5- and 6-oxygen polyethers the alkali-metal cation may also be coordinated to water molecules or anions, but with a 10-oxygen polyether the metal ion is coordinated only to the polyether. It has proved possible to achieve almost complete separation of potassium from caesium in methanol by preferential complex formation with a cyclic poly-ether. Similar complexes are formed by other polycyclic molecules containing both nitrogen and oxygen donor atoms. Other complex species, when they are formed, are found only in relatively concentrated solutions, the stability of the complex increasing with decreasing size of the anion. This is the expected order if electrostatic attraction is the major factor in the binding of the complexes. A parallel can be drawn between the oxo-anions that form weak acids and the stabilities of the corresponding complexes of the group IA cations, indicating that the behaviour of the proton in aqueous solution is similar to that of the small cation. Conversely the stability of complexes with anions of strong acids increases with increasing size of the cation (Table 11).

TABLE 11

Stability constants ($lg K_1$) of some complexes of group IA cations

	Li	Na	K	Rb	Cs
OH^-	0·2	−0·6	—	—	—
Cl^-	—	—	—	−0·77	−0·5
SO_4^{2-}	0·6	0·7	0·96	—	—
$EDTA^{4-}$	2·7	1·7	—	—	—

($EDTA^{4-}$ = ethylenediaminetetra-acetate)

Ion-association reactions are favoured by a decrease in the permittivity of the medium, as noted previously (p. 6), and this may lead to the forma-tion of either outer-sphere or inner-sphere complexes. The complex

$K^+[Na(NH_2)_2]^-$ may be precipitated from liquid ammonia, and complexes of Li^+, Na^+, or K^+ with the sulphate or salicylate anion are produced in alcohol solution.

Hydrated-ion size

The smaller the cation the greater will be the interaction with water: this is represented by the solvation enthalpy of the cations. Lithium, which has the smallest crystal radius of the alkali cations, is strongly solvated in water. The extent of the hydration is not confined to the coordination sphere alone and additional layers of water molecules are attached, but with decreasing strength of attraction. The net result is that the cation with the smallest crystal radius has the largest hydrated radius. If, for example, a mixture of alkali-metal cations is eluted from an ion-exchange column the order of elution is lithium, sodium, potassium, rubidium, and caesium. Since the cations are bound to the resin by electrostatic forces, and the lithium cation is the least strongly bound, this implies that in solution it has the largest effective radius.

The hydrogen cation

Hydrogen is the only non-metal to form a simple cationic species that is stable in solution. Since this is a singly-charged ion it is convenient to discuss it at this stage. The ionization potential $H(g) \rightarrow H^+(g)$ at $1310\,kJ\,mol^{-1}$ is considerably higher than the corresponding ionization potential of lithium. As a result hydrogen differs from lithium in that its bonds to other elements are mainly covalent. The hydrogen ion can only be obtained in solvents which readily solvate the proton: the high solvation energy of the very small cation is mainly responsible for the ionization (p. 5). The transfer of the solvated ion between two species in solution is responsible for acid–base behaviour (p. 27). Strong acids are highly dissociated in solution, indicating that the $H_3O^+(aq)$ ion has little affinity for the anions of strong acids, such as Cl^-, ClO_4^-, and NO_3^-. However, the existence of weak acids such as HCN and NH_4^+ in aqueous solution indicates a larger affinity for the more polarizable species. The H_3O^+ ion may be obtained in crystalline hydrates of a number of acids. Thus the hydrates of the hydrogen halides $HX \cdot H_2O$ contain $H_3O^+X^-$, and $HClO_4 \cdot H_2O$ contains $H_3O^+ClO_4^-$ which is isomorphous with $NH_4^+ClO_4^-$.

Group IIA

Solubility

The salts of strong acids are soluble, with the notable exception of the sulphates of calcium, strontium, and barium. The salts of the weak acids show a considerable decline in solubility, with hydroxides, fluorides, carbonates, and oxalates in general having low solubilities for Mg^{2+}, Ca^{2+}, Sr^{2+}, and Ba^{2+}. The relative order of solubility varies with the anion. This change from solubility of salts of strong acids to insolubility of salts of weak acids is much more pronounced than with the alkali metals, although lithium has some tendency to this behaviour. All the hydroxides, with the exception of beryllium hydroxide, are strong bases, but are considerably less soluble than the corresponding alkali-metal compounds. Beryllium hydroxide is amphoteric, dissolving in acids to produce the tetra-aquoberyllium ion.

TABLE 12

Some properties of the group IIA metals

	Be	Mg	Ca	Sr	Ba
Ionic radius/nm	0·038	0·066	0·099	0·115	0·137
Ionization potentials/ (kJ mol^{-1})					
First	895	734	587	541	500
Second	1746	1443	1140	1059	959
Standard electrode potential/(V)	−1·85	−2·37	−2·87	−2·89	−2.90
Enthalpy of hydration/ (kJ mol^{-1})	—	1924	1580	1485	1276

Hydrolysis

The increase in charge and decrease in size compared with the adjacent elements in group IA leads to an increase in the polarizing power of the cations. In the case of Be^{2+} the high charge density on the ion is sufficient to produce hydrolysis of beryllium salts in aqueous solution, but in acid solutions the hydrated ion $Be(H_2O)_4^{2+}$ is present. Because of this high affinity for water molecules the Be^{2+} ion is the most heavily hydrated of all the divalent ions, although the heat of hydration of the beryllium ion is apparently unable to compensate for the high sublimation energy and ionization potential of beryllium. Thus the order of electrode potentials in group IIA is different from the order in group IA (see Tables 10 and 12). The tetra-aquoberyllium ion is also obtained in the solid phase, and the stability of the hydrated ion is demonstrated by the fact that $\{Be(H_2O)_4\}(ClO_4)_2$ can be heated to decomposition without loss of water. The other members of group IIA have a decreasing affinity for water and not even the magnesium ion, probably present as $Mg(H_2O)_6^{2+}$, shows any acidity or tendency to hydrolysis. The magnesium ion still has a considerable affinity for water, however, and anhydrous magnesium perchlorate is used as a drying agent.

The important feature of the $Be(H_2O)_4^{2+}$ ion is its readiness to hydrolyse. From studies of the concentration of base required to cause precipitation it is suggested that a soluble hydrolytic species is first produced, with a structure

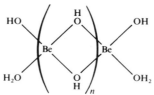

where the beryllium achieves the usual coordination number of four by coordination of extra water molecules. Similar hydroxy-bridges are present in the colloidal particles formed before precipitation and in gelatinous beryllium hydroxide:

Addition of alkali first displaces the water molecules at the ends of the chain, but at higher alkali concentrations the hydroxy-bridges are progressively broken down. The process should lead eventually to the formation of the mononuclear beryllate anion, $\{Be(OH)_4\}^{2-}$ but even with a Na_2O/BeO mol ratio of 14:1 the predominant beryllate species contains ten beryllium atoms. The observed solubility of beryllium oxide in aqueous solutions of beryllium salts can also be interpreted in these terms. The addition of beryllium oxide changes the beryllium concentration and the pH, factors which increase the hydrolytic polymerization of the hydrated Be^{2+} ion (p. 21).

Complex ions

The large polarizing power of the small Be^{2+} ion, which results in the hydrolysis of the aquo ions, also favours complex formation. The Be^{2+} ion would be classified as a hard acid, so the fact that the majority of complexes are formed with hard bases, particularly with oxygen donor atoms, is to be expected. A saturated aqueous solution of beryllium fluoride contains the species BeF^+, BeF_2, BeF_3^-, and BeF_4^{2-}. The relative concentrations of these species depend on the F^-/Be^{2+} concentration ratio and on the pH.

The hard-acid character of the Be^{2+} ion is further demonstrated by the failure to prepare the chloroberyllate ion $BeCl_4^{2-}$ from aqueous solutions.

TABLE 13

Stability constants ($\lg K_1$) *of some complexes of group II A cations*

	Mg^{2+}	Ca^{2+}	Sr^{2+}	Ba^{2+}
OH^-	2·6	1·5	0·9	0·7
F^-	1·8	1·0	—	0·45
Cl^-	0·6	—	—	−0·13
$EDTA^{4-}$	9·12	11·0	8·6	7·8
Oxalate	2·8	3·0	2·5	2·3
Tartrate	1·4	2·8	1·9	2·5
SO_4^{2-}	2·2	2·3	—	—

The salts $M_2^I BeCl_4$ (where M^I is an alkali metal) can be obtained from anhydrous melts, but are readily hydrolysed. Thermally stable ammine complexes $[Be(NH_3)_4]X_2$ have been prepared but these are also readily hydrolysed.

The tendency to form complexes decreases down the group, as cation size increases. Possibly the most important group of complexes are those formed by ethylenediaminetetra-acetate ($EDTA^{4-}$); e.g. $Ca^{2+}(aq) + EDTA^{4-} \rightarrow Ca(EDTA)^{2-}$. This reaction is the basis of the complexometric titration method. The end point is given by the displacement of a coordinated indicator from the cation to form the more stable EDTA complex. The stability of the complexes decreases in the order $Ca^{2+} > Mg^{2+} \sim Sr^{2+} > Ba^{2+}$. The lower stability of the Mg^{2+} complexes compared with Ca^{2+} and Sr^{2+} is due mainly to an unfavourable enthalpy term: the order of decreasingly favourable enthalpies is $Ca^{2+} > Ba^{2+} > Sr^{2+} \gg Mg^{2+}$. This is the net result of electrostatic binding energies, which are greatest with small cations, and steric crowding, which is also greatest with the small cations. In the case of the small Mg^{2+} ion the difficulty in accommodating the four carboxylate and the two amine groups of the $EDTA^{4-}$ ion is the dominating factor. The manner in which $EDTA^{4-}$ is coordinated to a metal ion is shown in Fig. 6. The formation of six five-membered rings is presumably responsible for the stability of the complex but with a small cation the steric crowding reduces the stability.

Smaller monodentate ligands, water, for example, can be arranged more easily around the ions and then the enthalpies decrease uniformly with increasing size. The formation of complexes between ions of opposite charge arises largely from the favourable entropy change which accompanies the loss of hydration. It is this term which is mainly responsible for complex formation by the cations of groups IA and IIA. The hydrated cation produces ordering of the solvent, an effect which is greater with small, highly-charged cations. When complex formation occurs this hydration of the cation is lost with a resulting increase in the disorder of the system.

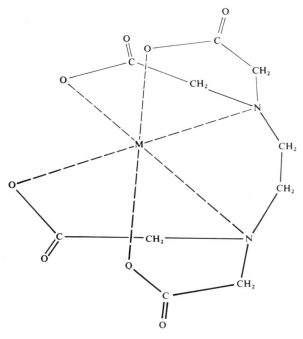

Fig. 6. Metal complex with the ethylenediamine tetra-acetate anion.

Calcium and magnesium ions form important complexes with other oxygen-donor molecules. The long-chain alkyl sulphonates, which are used as detergents, and the long-chain alkyl carboxylates, the traditional soaps, give stable complexes with magnesium and calcium. Consequently the effectiveness of detergents and soaps is considerably reduced in solutions containing these metal ions; this phenomenon is very obvious in 'hard water' areas. One point of interest is that the interaction of the metal ions is greater with long-chain compounds than with the simple carboxylate or sulphonate molecules. The interference of the magnesium and calcium ions may be avoided by forming complexes of greater stability with soluble linear polyphosphate compounds; polyphosphates are widely used as water softeners. Ion-exchange resins containing polystyrenesulphonates also complex strongly with the group IA and group IIA cations, and may be used as water softeners or for the preparation of de-ionized water.

PROBLEMS

5.1. What ions are formed in dilute aqueous solutions of sodium chloride, magnesium chloride, aluminium chloride, and silicon tetrachloride?

5.2. The lattice energies of LiF, NaF, KF, RbF, and CsF are 1000, 890, 795, 760, and 725 kJ mol^{-1} respectively. The enthalpy of hydration of F^- is 515 kJ mol^{-1} and the enthalpies of hydration of the cations are given in Table 10. What relative order of solubility would you predict from these data for the alkali-metal fluorides? A saturated aqueous solution of LiF contains approximately 0·1 mol dm^{-3} but a saturated aqueous solution of NaF contains approximately 1 mol dm^{-3}. Explain this observation.

5.3. The solubility product of MgF_2 is $7·1 \times 10^{-9}$ mol^3 dm^{-9}. What is the solubility of magnesium fluoride in mol dm^{-3}? If the acid dissociation constant of hydrofluoric acid is $7·2 \times 10^{-4}$ mol dm^{-3} what is the solubility of magnesium fluoride in aqueous solution at constant pH = 2?

5.4. What chemical reactions in solution will distinguish between (a) Li^+ and K^+ (b) Mg^{2+} and Ca^{2+} (c) Be^{2+} and Ba^{2+}?

5.5. Write an expression for K_h, the hydrolysis constant of Be^{2+}, and show that it is directly related to K_b, the base dissociation constant of $BeOH^+$. If $K_b = 10^{-8}$ mol dm^{-3} what is the value of K_h?

5.6. 25 cm^3 of a solution containing calcium and magnesium ions requires 32.5 cm^3 of 0·01M EDTA at pH 9 for complete reaction. 25 cm^3 of the same solution requires 20 cm^3 of EDTA at pH 12 for complete reaction. Calculate the individual concentrations of Ca^{2+} and Mg^{2+} in the solution. The solubility product of $Mg(OH)_2$ is $1·2 \times 10^{-11}$ mol^3 dm^{-9}.

6. The elements of group IIIA, the lanthanides, and the actinides

Electronic configuration

THE chemistry of boron, the first member of group III, is that of a typical non-metallic element (see p. 77). Aluminium, the next member of the group, has a larger atomic radius and this results in a lower ionization potential and lower polarizing power of the M^{3+} cation. Aluminium and the larger members of the group therefore behave primarily as metals.

The aluminium ion, like the group IA and the group IIA cations, has the electronic configuration of the preceding noble gas. In this respect it is similar to scandium, yttrium, lanthanum, and actinium but different from gallium, indium, and thallium. The latter trio of elements contain filled d- and f-shells which have a significant effect on their chemistry. These elements are considered with the other metals which occur after the transition series.

TABLE 14

Some properties of the group IIIA metals

	Al	Sc	Y	La	Ac
Ionic radius/(nm)	0·052	0·081	0·092	0·114	0·118
Ionization potentials/ (kJ mol^{-1})					
First	577·5	631	615·5	541	—
Second	1809	1235	1187	1099	—
Third	2732	2387	1968	1849	—
Standard electrode potential/V	−1·67	−1·88	−2·37	−2·52	−2·6
Enthalpy of hydration/ (kJ mol^{-1})	4690	—	—	—	—
pK_a	5	6	8	10	—

Lanthanum is the first member of a series of fourteen elements in which the 4f orbital is progressively filled. This shell lies inside the filled 5s and 5p orbitals, which are outermost in the M^{3+} ion: changes in the population of the 4f shell have little effect on the chemistry of the ions. There is a progressive decrease in size across the series (in accord with the observation that size decreases across any horizontal series in the periodic table) with a total shrinkage of 0·021 nm. Since neighbouring ions of the same charge have radii differing by only about 0·002 nm their chemistry shows considerable similarity. A comparable series of elements follows actinium, where the 5f shell is considered to be filled progressively. However, it appears that the 5f orbitals are not stable relative to the 6d orbitals for the first few members of the series, in contrast to the stability of the 4f orbitals relative to the 5d. The energies of the 5f and 6d orbitals are also closer to the higher s- and p-orbitals (7s, 7p) than is the case for the lanthanide series. As a result the actinide elements can more readily form covalent bonds, and complex compounds, than can the lanthanides. For further discussion see Puddephatt (1972).

Solubility and hydrolysis

The salts of the M^{3+} ions with anions of strong acids are usually soluble. Aluminium salts of the weak acids are readily hydrolysed to the insoluble hydroxide. The extent of the hydrolysis will depend on the base strength of the anion. For example, acetate is a weaker base than carbonate and aluminium acetate is hydrolysed to the basic acetate but aluminium carbonate is completely hydrolysed to the hydrated oxide. Scandium salts also have a tendency to hydrolyse, though it is less pronounced than with aluminium. The basicity of the metal ions shows the expected increase with size, and yttrium, lanthanum, and actinium salts are progressively less easily hydrolysed. A similar trend is maintained across the lanthanide series; a decrease in size and increasing acidity results in hydrolysis of the heavier lanthanide carbonates, whereas the lighter lanthanide hydroxides are sufficiently basic to absorb carbon dioxide.

In acid solution the aluminium ion is present as the hexa-aquo ion, but coordination numbers higher than six are possible with the lanthanides, where the ions $Ln(H_2O)_9^{3+}$ and $Ln(H_2O)_8^{3+}$ are known in the solid state. Hydrolysis of perchloric acid solutions containing the M^{3+} cation produces polymeric ions, the nature of which depends on pH and metal-ion concentration, e.g.

$$2Al^{3+} + 2H_2O \rightarrow [Al_2(OH)_2]^{4+} + 2H^+$$

$$13Al^{3+} + 32H_2O \rightarrow [Al_{13}(OH)_{32}]^{7+} + 32H^+$$

The pH at which precipitation occurs increases with the size of the ion. Only aluminium and to a lesser extent scandium exhibit amphoteric properties. The hydroxides readily dissolve in concentrated sodium hydroxide, and although the nature of the species present in the solution is not known a comparison with the behaviour of beryllium suggests that a range of polymeric species will be present.

Complex ions

Complex formation is confined almost entirely to ligands containing oxygen donor atoms and to the halide ions (Table 15). Aluminium gives all six fluoro-complexes, AlF^{2+} to AlF_6^{3-}, in solution, but only the tetrahedral complex ions

TABLE 15

Stability constants ($\lg K_1$) of some complexes of M^{3+} cations

	Al^{3+}	Sc^{3+}	Y^{3+}	La^{3+}	Lu^{3+}
F^-	6·4	7·1	4·8	3·6	—
Cl^-	—	0·95	1·3	−0·1	1·45
OH^-	9·0	8·0	7·0	5·0	8·0
$EDTA^{4-}$	16·1	23·1	17·8	15·4	19·0

are formed with the heavier halogens, and these complexes are readily hydrolysed in water. They are however important as intermediates in Friedel–Crafts reactions in non-aqueous solvents.

$$R \cdot COCl + AlCl_3 \rightarrow RCO^+ + AlCl_4^-$$

$$R \cdot CO^+ + C_6H_6 \rightarrow R \cdot CO \cdot C_6H_5 + H^+$$

Scandium similarly forms fluoro-complexes, and scandium fluoride is soluble in solutions containing fluoride ions. The complex ions $ScCl^{2+}$ and $ScCl_2^+$ are known in perchloric acid solution. The formation constants of these complexes may be compared with the corresponding formation constants for indium chloro-complexes under identical conditions. These demonstrate that factors other than ionic size and charge are responsible for the stability of the B-group elements. The lanthanides form only weak fluoro-complexes and

TABLE 16

Stability constants of Sc^{3+} and In^{3+} with chloride ion

	Sc^{3+}	In^{3+}
Ionic size/nm	0·081	0·081
$\lg K_1$	0·04	2·36
$\lg K_2$	−0·15	1·27
$\lg K_3$	no complex	0·3

The values of $\lg K_1$ in this table were obtained using conditions (293 K and 0·69M $HClO_4$) different from those used for $\lg K_1$ in Table 15.

consequently the fluorides are only slightly soluble in aqueous solution of fluoride ion. As is to be expected the tendency to form fluoro-complexes increases with decreasing size of the lanthanide ion. This dependence of complex stability on ion size illustrates the importance of ionic bonding in these complexes, and this order is observed with other weak-acid oxo-anions. The reverse effect is observed with strong-acid oxo-anions, so that yttrium and lanthanum form sulphate complexes, which are not known for aluminium and scandium. The important complexes with oxygen donor atoms are those that contain chelate rings. The neutral complexes are insoluble in water but anionic complexes are soluble and may be isolated as salts of large cations.

Separation of lanthanides and actinides

The order of elution from an ion-exchange column depends on the hydrated ion size (p. 40). Thus the lanthanides will be eluted from the column in reverse order of atomic number—lutetium first, lanthanum last. The degree of separation achieved in this way is small because of the small difference in size. Increased separation is obtained by eluting the ions from the column with a complexing agent, usually an oxo-anion of a weak acid, such as citrate. As noted above the stability of these complexes increases with decreasing ionic radius, so complex formation will be greater with Lu^{3+} than with La^{3+}. This

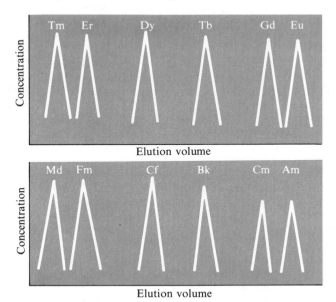

Fig. 7. A comparison of the ion-exchange separation of the lanthanides and the actinides.

supplements the greater tendency of the hydrated Lu^{3+} ion to pass into the solution, and increases the degree of separation.

The separation of individual actinide elements requires a preliminary separation of the actinide group from lanthanide ions. The mixture of ions is adsorbed on to an ion-exchange resin and eluted with strong hydrochloric acid solution. The larger actinides form chloro-complexes more readily, and so pass into solution and are eluted from the column. The actinide ions may be separated from each other in an analogous manner to that used for the lanthanides. Not only does the order of elution follow the same pattern, but the spacings between the eluted ions are remarkably similar when corresponding ions in the two series are compared.

Oxidation states other than + 3

At the beginning of the lanthanide series the difference in energy between the 4f electrons and the 5d electrons is small, with the 4f electrons increasing in stability across the series as the nuclear charge increases. Only cerium loses a 4f electron at all readily, to give the M^{4+} ion which is stable in aqueous solution. The highly-charged ion will have a marked tendency to hydrolyse, and the aquo-ion $[Ce(H_2O)_n]^{4+}$ will be a strong acid (pK_a -0.85). The aquo-ion will be present only in strong perchloric acid solutions; in other strong acid solutions coordination will occur with the anion of the acid. This is reflected in the electrode potentials for Ce^{4+}, Ce^{3+} in different acids: $E = 1.28$ V in 2 M HCl, 1.44 V in 1 M H_2SO_4, 1.61 V in 0.5–2 M HNO_3, and 1.70 V in 1 M $HClO_4$.

Europium is the only lanthanide to form an appreciably stable M^{2+} ion in aqueous solution, and these solutions have reducing properties $E^{\ominus}_{Eu^{3+},Eu^{2+}} = -0.43$ V). The Eu^{2+} ion shows some chemistry expected for an M^{2+} ion (Chapter 5) in that the hydroxide is soluble, and the sulphate and the chromate are insoluble. Europium metal dissolves in liquid ammonia with the formation of Eu^{2+} and solvated electrons.

TABLE 17

Oxidation states of the actinide elements

Ac	Th	Pa	U	Np	Pu	Am	Cm	Bk	Cf	Es	Fm	Md	No	Lw
													2	
3	3	3	3	3	3	**3**	3	3	3	3	3	3	**3**	**3**
	4	4	4	4	**4**	4	4	4						
		5	5	**5**	5	5								
			6	6	6	6								

The common oxidation state in aqueous solution is shown in bold type.

The early members of the actinide series have little energy difference between the 5f and the 6d orbitals. This leads to a marked tendency to remove both 6d and 5f electrons and produce ions with a noble-gas configuration. The stable oxidation states are thus Th(IV), Pa(V), and U(VI) which are comparable with oxidation states of the first members of the second and third transition series rather than with the lanthanides. However, the increasing stability of the 5f orbitals across the series leads to increased stability of the $+3$ oxidation state, and behaviour comparable with that of the lanthanides.

Ions in the oxidation states $+5$ and $+6$ occur as the oxo-cations MO_2^+ and MO_2^{2+} both in the solid state and in solution. The MO_2^{2+} ions, which are the more easily studied, have a linear structure and can persist through a variety of chemical changes. The chemistry of the ions is close to that of a small divalent ion such as Be^{2+}, rather than to the chemistry of a transition metal of similar charge and size. Thus stable complexes are formed with F^-, OH^-, SO_4^{2-}, and NO_3^-.

TABLE 18

Stability constants ($\lg K_1$) of cations in the actinide series

	Th^{4+}	U^{4+}	UO_2^{2+}	Pu^{3+}	Pu^{4+}
F^-	7·6	7·0	4·5		7·9
Cl^-	0·3	0·9	0·4	1·2	−0·3
SO_4^{2-}	3·3	3·6	3·0	1	3·7

Actinide ions in higher oxidation states exhibit the expected greater tendency to hydrolyse and to form complexes. For a given element the expected order would be $M^{4+} > MO_2^{2+} > M^{3+} > MO_2^+$. Complexes with F^- are more stable than complexes with Cl^-, and complexes with oxygen donor atoms are more stable than complexes with sulphur donor atoms. Such properties place these ions in the category of 'hard' acids. Complex formation may alter the relative stability of the different oxidation states of an actinide. The addition of sulphate ions to a solution of NpO_2^+ results in disproportionation to

TABLE 19

Standard electrode potentials ($E^\ominus/V$) of some actinide elements

	MO_2^{2+}, MO_2^+	MO_2^+, M^{4+}	M^{4+}, M^{3+}	M^{3+}, M
U	0·06	0·58	−0·63	−1·8
Np	1·14	0·74	0·16	−1·83
Pu	0·91	1·17	0·98	−2·03
Am	1·6	1·04	2·7	−2·32

Np^{4+} and NpO_2^{2+}. This occurs because of the above order of stability of the different complex ions. Disproportionation would not be expected in the absence of complexing ions (Table 19). Complexing reactions will not be significant in perchloric acid solution, so that changes in pH and metal-ion concentration will produce polymeric species containing oxo- or hydroxo-groups of the general type already described (p. 22).

PROBLEMS

6.1. 25 cm^3 of a solution containing 33·3 g dm^{-3} of potassium hexacyanoferrate(II) requires 19·7 cm^3 of 0·1M cerium(IV) solution for oxidation. (a) What is the percentage of Fe(II) in the complex? (b) The electrode potential $E_{Ce^{4+},Ce^{3+}}$ is 1·44 V. What is the equilibrium constant for this reaction? (c) If Fe^{2+}(aq) is used instead of the cyano-complex what is the equilibrium constant for this reaction? Refer to Table 26 for the electrode potentials.

6.2. Explain the reactions which occur when an aqueous solution of (a) sodium carbonate and (b) sodium hydroxide is added to an aqueous solution of aluminium ions.

6.3. In the lanthanide series the pH at which precipitation of the hydroxide occurs decreases from La^{3+} to Yb^{3+}. Explain this observation.

6.4. Which metal is the stronger reducing agent in acid solution, aluminium or gallium? Compare this relative order with that of sodium and potassium, and magnesium and calcium.

6.5. The equilibrium constant in acid solution for the reaction $2Np(v) \rightleftharpoons Np(iv) + Np(vi)$ is 4×10^{-7}. What effect would the addition of (a) fluoride ions and (b) iodide ions have on this reaction?

6.6. The stability constant for the reaction $Sc^{3+}(aq) + HF(aq) \rightleftharpoons ScF^{2+}(aq) + H^+(aq)$ is $10^{6·2}$. What proportion of a dilute solution of scandium ions are present as ScF^{2+}(aq) in 0·1M HF(aq) at constant pH = 2?

7. The metals of the B subgroups

Electronic configuration

THE elements which occur in the subgroups immediately following the transition elements show considerable difference in character from the elements already discussed. The filling of the d-orbitals in the transition series is accompanied by a corresponding increase in the nuclear charge, and the penetrating properties of the ns and np orbitals result in the electrons in these orbitals experiencing a marked increase in effective nuclear charge. This is even more pronounced after the third transition series where, in addition to the filling of 5d orbitals, the 4f orbitals have been filled in the lanthanide series (see Fig. 5). As a consequence the energy required to remove the ns and np electrons, which are the electrons also removed in the formation of the pre-transition cations, shows a pronounced increase. One additional effect arises from the greater penetrating properties of ns electrons compared with np. The ns electrons become more stable relative to the np, so that ions are produced in which the np electrons have been removed but the ns electrons are still present. The element will then have two oxidation states, one corresponding to the removal of all ns and np electrons, and one corresponding to the removal of the np electrons only.

Polarization effects

The increase in nuclear charge produces a marked increase in the ionization potentials. This effect may be seen by comparing the ionization potentials of group IIA and IIIA with the ionization potentials of IIB and IIIB. The large ionization potentials of the B-metals inevitably mean that the electron affinities of the cations will be increased, since this is the reverse of the ionization reaction. The increased electron affinities of these cations leads to a greater polarizing power than would be found for a cation of similar size and charge in the pre-transition metals. The overall result of these effects is that the B-metals form ions and compounds with the more electronegative elements less readily than the pre-transition metals. On the other hand the cations have a greater tendency to combine with polarizable anions or ligands. There is one further difference from the pre-transition elements in that there is often more than one oxidation state, namely the group oxidation state, N, and a lower oxidation state, $N-2$.

Complex ions

Complex stability decreases with increasing size of the cation within a given group of the pre-transition elements, and similarly the acidity of the aquo-ions steadily decreases. The B-metals do not exhibit such a uniform pattern of behaviour, and in a number of cases the order of stability of complexes is reversed, as is the acidity of the aquo-ions. These changes in behaviour may be attributed to the position of the elements in the periodic table after the transition elements, and the consequent effect on electron affinity that has already been described.

Group IIB: zinc, cadmium, and mercury

Solubility and hydrolysis

There is a close similarity in properties between zinc and cadmium, and in many cases a marked discontinuity between cadmium and mercury. The Zn^{2+} and Cd^{2+} ions are similar in many respects to Mg^{2+}, and have a number of isomorphous salts. The solubility pattern also resembles that of Mg^{2+} in that the halides with the exception of the fluoride are soluble, and in general the salts of strong oxo-acid anions are soluble, while the salts of the weak oxo-acid anions are insoluble. Unlike the magnesium aquo-ion, which is only weakly acidic ($pK_a = 12$), the zinc and cadmium aquo-ions are quite strong acids. The increased acidity arises from the greater interaction of the IIB cations with the water molecules, as demonstrated by the different heats of hydration of the Ca^{2+} ion ($r = 0.099$ nm, $-\Delta H = 1580$ kJ mol^{-1}) and the Cd^{2+} ion ($r = 0.096$ nm, $-\Delta H = 1805$ kJ mol^{-1}) although the size of the ions is similar.

The salts of strong oxo-acid anions with Hg^{2+} are soluble. However extensive hydrolysis will occur because mercury(II) hydroxide is a very weak base. Mercury(II) fluoride, a compound in which the anion is of low polarizability, behaves as an essentially ionic compound. The aqueous solution will, however, be even more extensively hydrolysed, since hydrogen fluoride is a weak acid. Mercury(II) chloride and cyanide dissolve in water but are only weakly dissociated, so that there is no appreciable hydrolysis.

Zinc hydroxide is amphoteric and will dissolve in excess alkali to form zincate ions, and the salts $NaZn(OH)_3$ and $Na_2Zn(OH)_4$ can be isolated from concentrated solutions. Although the structures of the ions in solution are not known definitely, possible species are $Zn(OH)_4^{2-}$, $[Zn(OH)_3H_2O]^-$, and $[Zn(OH)_3(H_2O)_3]^-$. Cadmium hydroxide is a stronger base and has no amphoteric character, this distinct increase in basic character is consistent with the trend observed with the pre-transition metals. Mercury(II) hydroxide is however an extremely weak base with some slight amphoteric character.

Complex ions

Complex compounds are formed by all three metal cations with chloride, bromide, and iodide, but there is no evidence for fluoromercury(II) complexes. The stability of the fluoro-complexes follows the same order as with pre-transition metal cations, but the order of stability of the complexes is reversed

TABLE 20

Some properties of the group IIB and group IIIB metals

	Zn	Cd	Hg	Ga	In	Tl(III)	Tl(I)
Ionic radius/nm	0.072	0.096	0.110	0.060	0.081	0.095	0.140
Covalent radius/nm	0.131	0.148	0.148	0.125	0.149	0.155	—
Ionization potentials/(kJ mol^{-1})							
First	906	867	1006	576	556	586	—
Second	1733	1631	1809	1971	1813	1960	—
Third	—	—	—	2952	2692	2866	—
Standard electrode potential/V	−0.76	−0.40	0.85	−0.52	−0.34	0.72	−0.34
Enthalpy of hydration/(kJ mol^{-1})	2056	1805	1845	4703	4159	4117	—
pK_a	9.0	9.1	—	2.6	3.7	1.2	—

TABLE 21

Stability constants (lg K_1) for some complexes of group IIB and group IIIB cations

	Zn^{2+}	Cd^{2+}	Hg^{2+}	Ga^{3+}	In^{3+}	Tl^{3+}	Tl^+
F^-	0.75	0.46	1.0	5.0	3.7	3.0	0.1
I^-	−2.93	2.96	13.5	<0.0	1.5	11.4	0.7
NH_3	2.2	2.5	8.8	—	—	—	−0.9
$EDTA^{4-}$	16.2	16.5	22.0	20.3	25.0	—	—

with the more polarizable anions. This change in soft acid character of the cation is demonstrated by the ionic species formed in aqueous solutions of the metal halides. Thus aqueous solutions of zinc chloride contain the ions $[Zn(H_2O)_6]^{2+}$ and $[ZnCl_4(H_2O)_2]^{2-}$ but there is no evidence for $[ZnCl_4]^{2-}$ or $[ZnCl_3]^-$. On the other hand an aqueous solution of cadmium bromide contains $[CdBr_4]^{2-}$, $[CdBr_3]^-$ and $[CdBr]^+$, but there is no evidence for $[Cd(H_2O)_n]^{2+}$. The complexes formed by the Hg^{2+} cation are usually more stable than those of any other divalent cation. Because of the marked tendency of the aquo-ions of these elements to hydrolyse, and because the other complex ions are so stable, only in strong acid solution containing weakly coordinating anions, such as perchlorate, will simple aquo-ions be the sole species present.

The Hg^{2+} cation forms 4-coordinate complexes but in addition has a pronounced tendency to form complexes with coordination number two. Formation constants for reactions with ammonia indicate that the first two

$$Hg^{2+} + 2NH_3 \rightleftharpoons Hg(NH_3)_2^{2+} \qquad K = 3.2 \times 10^{17} \, mol^{-2} \, dm^6$$

$$Hg(NH_3)_2^{2+} + 2NH_3 \rightleftharpoons Hg(NH_3)_4^{2+} \qquad K = 6 \times 10^1 \, mol^{-2} \, dm^6$$

ligands are held much more firmly than the second two. Similarly aqueous solutions of mercury(II) chloride contain predominantly $HgCl_2$ with only very little $[HgCl_4]^{2-}$ and $[HgCl_3]^-$. However, in the presence of excess halide ion the species $[HgX]^+$, HgX_2, $[HgX_3]^-$, and $[HgX_4]^{2-}$ are produced. The three cations all form four coordinate complexes with nitrogen donors, such as ammonia, in which the zinc complexes are slightly more stable than the cadmium complexes but much less stable than the mercury complexes. It is only with the larger more polarizable ligands that cadmium complexes become appreciably more stable than those of zinc. In general zinc prefers donor atoms from the first short period—O, N, and F—while cadmium and mercury prefer the heavier donor atoms from these groups—S, P, and Br.

The mercury(I) ion

In aqueous solution the mercury(II) ion reacts rapidly with mercury to establish the equilibrium $Hg^{2+} + Hg \rightleftharpoons Hg_2^{2+}$; $K = 166$.

The standard potentials for the two mercury ions are

$$Hg_2^{2+} + 2e^- = 2Hg(s) \qquad E^{\ominus} = 0.789 \text{ V}$$

$$Hg^{2+} + 2e^- = Hg(s) \qquad E^{\ominus} = 0.854 \text{ V}$$

indicating that the formation of Hg_2^{2+} directly without the parallel formation of Hg^{2+} requires an oxidizing agent with a potential in the narrow range 0.79 to 0.85 V. The reaction between oxidizing agents and mercury will therefore almost invariably produce Hg^{2+}, but in the presence of at least 50 per cent excess mercury, Hg_2^{2+} will be the final product.

The Hg_2^{2+} is the only stable cation of its kind in aqueous solution. It has an Hg—Hg bond distance of 0.25 nm, compared with 0.31 nm in the metal, despite the presence of the charges. The cation combines with no more than two groups, unlike other M(I) cations which have higher coordination numbers, particularly with unsaturated donors. Although the Cd_2^{2+} ion may be isolated from a reaction in a molten salt it disproportionates immediately in aqueous solution.

The main soluble and stable salts of mercury(I) are the nitrate, the chlorate, and the perchlorate. The mercury(I) ion has a smaller affinity than the mercury(II) ion for hydroxide and sulphide, so the above equilibrium is displaced to the left when these anions are added to solutions of mercury(I) salts. Addition of CN^- also causes disproportionation; the $Hg(CN)_2$ remains in solution but is only weakly dissociated. Complex formation is limited to oxygen-donor ligands of low polarizability, such as oxalate, $C_2O_4^{2-}$, and tripolyphosphate, $P_3O_{10}^{5-}$. The complexes formed with almost all other ligands are less stable than the corresponding complexes of mercury(II), so that attempted complex formation also results in disproportionation.

Group IIIB: gallium, indium, and thallium

Solubility and hydrolysis

Salts of strong oxo-acid anions are usually soluble, but salts of weak acids are unstable in the presence of water, because of extensive hydrolysis of the cations. The acidity of the M^{3+} aquo-ions is greater than the acidity of the M^{2+} ions of group IIB, as might be expected with the increase in charge and decrease in size, and in the group Tl^{3+}(aq) has the highest acidity. Gallium hydroxide resembles aluminium hydroxide in its amphoteric properties, dissolving in excess alkali to give gallate species of the probable form $[Ga(OH)_4]^-$ or $[Ga(OH)_4(H_2O)_2]^-$. Indium hydroxide has no amphoteric properties and is entirely basic in character. There is no hydroxide of thallium(III), but the oxide Tl_2O_3 is entirely basic in character.

Complex ions

The halide complexes formed by the metal ions demonstrate the increasingly 'soft' character of the metal ion down the group. In aqueous solution six-coordinate gallium fluoro-complexes of the type $[GaF_6]^{3-}$ and $[GaF_5H_2O]^{2-}$ are stable, as are the tetrahedral $[GaCl_4]^-$ species, while for thallium(III) tetrabromo- and tetraiodo-complexes are known, but not the fluoro-complex. The other main group of complexes contains the oxygen-donor ligands, particularly chelate groups such as oxalate and 8-hydroxyquinoline. Ammonia and amines do not form complexes in aqueous solution, because of the extensive hydrolysis of the aquo ions.

The thallium(I) ion

This is the only metal in the group to give a stable M^+ ion in aqueous solution. Tl^+ behaves very much like a cation of group IA in forming a soluble oxide, hydroxide, cyanide, and carbonate, while the nitrate, perchlorate, and sulphate are isomorphous with the potassium salts. However, thallium(I) bromate, iodate, sulphide, and the halides, except the fluoride are only sparingly soluble. In this respect the Tl^+ cation shows a closer resemblance to Ag^+ than to the alkali metals. Like the alkali-metal cations Tl^+ has little tendency to hydrolyse, in which respect it differs markedly from Tl^{3+} which is extensively hydrolysed even at pH 1–2·5.

Complex formation is limited to halo-complexes and complexes with oxygen and sulphur ligands. One result of the difference in stability between Tl^+ and Tl^{3+} complexes is that the electrode potential for the process $Tl^{3+} + 2e^- = Tl^+$ will depend on pH and on the presence of complexing anions. Thus $E^{\ominus}$ is $+1·26$ V in 1 M $HClO_4$ but falls to $+0·77$ V in 1 M HCl owing to formation of stronger chloro-complexes of Tl^{3+}.

Group IVB: germanium, tin, and lead

Solubility and hydrolysis

Within the group only tin and lead can be considered as metals; germanium is intermediate in character between metal and non-metal. When the cations have the group oxidation state the resulting high charge and small size will give a strong polarizing power. Of the known tetrahalides only tin(IV) fluoride and lead(IV) fluoride can be considered as ionic in character and the covalent type halides will undergo extensive hydrolysis. In strong-acid solution the hydrolysis may be suppressed, so that germanium chloride and bromide solutions contain species of the general form $[Ge(OH)_nX_{6-n}]^{2-}$. Tin(IV) chloride under similar conditions gives solutions containing $SnCl_6^{2-}$ and $SnCl_5^-$ species. There are very few salts of oxo-acids; even the salts of strong oxo-acids which can be prepared, tin(IV) sulphate for example, are extensively hydrolysed in aqueous solution (p. 20).

The basicity of the oxides increases down the group. GeO_2 is mainly acidic, but will dissolve in concentrated hydrochloric acid to form the tetrachloride; SnO_2 is amphoteric; PbO_2 has little solubility in dilute acid or base, and so is

TABLE 22
Some properties of the group IVB and group VB metals

	Ge(IV)	Sn(IV)	Sn(II)	Pb(IV)	Pb(II)	Sb(III)	Bi(III)
Ionic radius/nm	0.053	0.071	0.110	0.084	0.127	0.092	0.108
Covalent radius/nm	0.122		0.141		0.154	0.141	0.152
Ionization potentials/(kJ mol^{-1})							
First	780	704		712		835	772
Second	1530	1399		1443		1737	1602
Third	3290	2943		3078		2383	2451
Fourth	4389	3801		4062			
Standard electrode potential/V			−0.143		−0.138		
pK$_a$							

not well characterized. The oxides of tin and lead combine with strong bases to form stannates and plumbates, which contain the anions $M(OH)_6^{2-}$. Complex formation by the cation is almost entirely confined to these halo- and hydroxo-complexes.

The divalent cations

The divalent state becomes increasingly stable with respect to the group oxidation state with increasing atomic weight. This is reflected by aqueous

TABLE 23

Standard electrode potentials ($E^{\ominus}/V$) of group IVB and group VB metals

Acid solution		Basic solution	
GeO_2, Ge^{2+}	-0.3	$Sn(OH)_6^{2-}, HSnO_2^-$	-0.93
Sn^{4+}, Sn^{2+}	0.15	$HSnO_2^-, Sn$	-0.91
PbO_2, Pb^{2+}	1.45	PbO_2, PbO	0.28
		PbO, Pb	-0.54

solutions of Sn(II) which are mild reducing agents, whereas Pb(II) solutions are not. That the divalent cation has increased metallic character is shown by the more extensive range of salts which are formed, and there are some resemblances to the cations of group IIB. As a general rule the salts of strong oxo-acids are soluble, with the exception of lead sulphate, while the salts of weak oxo-acids are insoluble. The important tin(II) halides are the chloride and fluoride, which in aqueous solution readily combine with halide ion to form SnX_3^-. The order of stability of the tin(II)–halide complexes is $F^- > Cl^- > Br^- > I^-$ while the reverse order is found for lead(II)–halide complexes. As a general rule the stability constants of many Pb^{2+} complexes are closely

TABLE 24

Stability constants ($\lg K_1$) for some complexes of group IVB and group VB cations

	Sn^{2+}	Pb^{2+}	Sb^{3+}	Bi^{3+}
F^-	3.0	0.5	—	—
Cl^-	1.5	1.2	2.3	2.2
Br^-	1.1	1.5	—	2.3
OH^-	—	7.5	—	—
$EDTA^{4-}$	—	17.5	—	—
I^-	—	—	—	3.63

in line with those of Cd^{2+}. The Pb^{2+} cation forms chloro-complexes of the general form $PbCl_n^{(2-n)+}$, but $PbCl_6^{4-}$ is formed only at high concentrations of added Cl^-. Although the tin(II) and lead(II) complexes are comparable up to $n = 4$, there is no evidence for tin(II) complexes with $n > 4$.

The main product of the hydrolysis of Sn(II) is $Sn_3(OH)_4^{2+}$ and the equilibrium constant for the reaction $3Sn^{2+} + 4H_2O \rightleftharpoons Sn_3(OH)_4^{2+} + 4H^+$ is $K = 10^{-6.77}$. A comparable polymeric species is obtained as a precipitate $Sn_4(OH)_6Cl_2$ from tin(II) chloride solution. Ion-exchange measurements on the saturated solution immediately before precipitation indicate the presence of $Sn_3(OH)_4^{2+}$ and $Sn(OH)_2Cl_2^{2-}$, which suggests that the precipitate contains both cationic and anionic tin complexes. Perchloric acid solutions of Pb(II) contain unhydrolysed and uncomplexed metal ions. With increasing basicity of the solutions the species present are formulated as $[Pb_4(OH)_4(ClO_4)_2]^{2+}$ and $[Pb_6(OH)_8(ClO_4)_3]^+$.

There is no evidence for the formation of ammine complexes in aqueous solution, because of the great affinity for OH^- which leads to ready hydrolysis.

Tin(II) and lead(II) oxides are both soluble in alkali to give stannate(II) and plumbate(II) species. The stannate(II) solutions are strongly reducing and in very concentrated alkalis disproportionate to tin and stannate(IV). Plumbate solutions are stable towards oxidation.

Group VB: arsenic, antimony, and bismuth

The elements of the group exhibit little metallic character in the group oxidation state, and only a limited number of ions are known. Antimony forms six coordinate ions MX_6^-, where $X = F^-$, Cl^-, or OH^-, in aqueous solution. In acetonitrile $SbCl_5$ ionizes to $SbCl_4^+$ and Cl^- in dilute solution but to $SbCl_4^+$ and $SbCl_6^-$ in concentrated solution.

Even in the lower oxidation state $+3$, arsenic has virtually no metallic character. It is precipitated from acid solution by hydrogen sulphide, in which it resembles the weakly basic oxides of the B-metals, with their preferred affinity for S as opposed to O. A few antimony(III) salts are known, but in aqueous solution they are extensively hydrolysed to the antimonyl ion, formulated as SbO^+. Antimony trichloride is stable in concentrated aqueous solution, but SbOCl is precipitated when the solution is diluted. The hydrolysis is suppressed by addition of acid or by the addition of Cl^- ions. Although there is no evidence for the formation of a true oxo-cation, SbO^+ has a superficial resemblance to the B-metal M^+ cations in that the halides have low solubility. Antimony(III) oxide is amphoteric, dissolving in bases to give the antimonite ion $Sb(OH)_4^-$, and these solutions containing the $Sb(OH)_4^-$ ion are strongly reducing. There are a number of anionic antimony complexes corresponding to the substitution of the OH^- groups.

The increase in metallic character continues with bismuth, for which there is extensive cationic chemistry of bismuth(III). The oxide is entirely basic and reacts with acids to form salts containing the bismuthyl ion BiO^+. Bismuth trichloride dissolves in water but is slowly hydrolysed to $BiOCl$. However $BiOCl$ will dissolve in hydrochloric acid from which the salt $(Me_4N)_3Bi_2Cl_9$ may be obtained. The solubility of this salt with change of Cl^- concentration has been studied, and interpreted in terms of the species $BiCl_4^-$ and $BiCl_6^{3-}$ in solution. There is no evidence for $BiCl_5^{2-}$. These chloro-complexes are more stable than the $PbCl_n^{(2-n)+}$ species but show the same preference for an even number of ligands.

In acid or neutral solution, in the absence of coordinating ions, there is a well-defined aquo-cation $[Bi_6(OH)_{12}]^{6+}$ (or $[Bi_6O_6]^{6+}$), while the species $[Bi_6O_6(OH)_3]^{3+}$ is formed at higher pH.

PROBLEMS

7.1. An aqueous solution containing 10^{-2} mol dm^{-3} of zinc nitrate is saturated with H_2S. The minimum pH at which zinc sulphide precipitates is 1·0. If potassium cyanide is added to give a concentration of 1 mol dm^{-3} then there is no precipitation below pH = 9. What is the overall stability constant of $Zn(CN)_4^{2-}$?

7.2. When a solution of $Bi(NO_3)_3$ in concentrated HCl was diluted a white precipitate appeared which redissolved on further addition of concentrated HCl. Explain this observation.

7.3. From the electrode potentials $E^{\ominus}_{Tl^+,Tl} = -0.34$ V and $E^{\ominus}_{Tl^{3+},Tl^+} = 1.25$ V calculate the equilibrium constant for the reaction $3Tl^+ \rightleftharpoons 2Tl + Tl^{3+}$. Will the Tl^+ ion disproportionate in aqueous solution?

7.4. A solution containing an ionized mercury(II) salt is in equilibrium with metallic mercury. The fraction of the dissolved mercury present as Hg(II) is independent of the concentration of Hg(I). Show that this agrees with the representation of mercury(I) ion as Hg_2^{2+} and not as Hg^+.

7.5. What chemical reactions in solution will distinguish between (a) Hg_2^{2+} and Hg^{2+} (b) Zn^{2+} and Cd^{2+} (c) Bi^{3+} and Sb^{3+} (d) Ga^{3+} and Tl^{3+}?

8. The transition metals

Electronic configuration

IN contrast to the metal ions so far considered, most transition-metal ions have a partly-filled $(n-1)$d shell of electrons which are in the surface region, i.e. at the periphery of the ion after the ionization of the ns^2 electrons; consequently they are influenced by surrounding ions or other ligands. The chemistry of the transition-metal ions will therefore depend on the number of d-electrons present and the way in which they are arranged. In this respect the transition elements differ from the lanthanides where the partly-filled f-shell is not at the periphery of the ion, and subsequent changes in filling of the f-shell have no great effect on the chemistry.

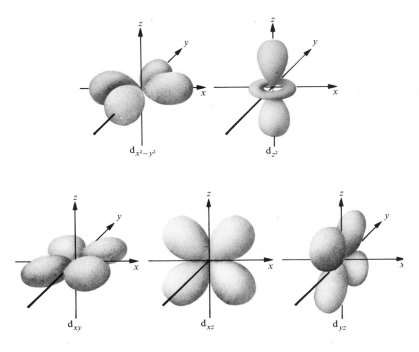

FIG. 8. Boundary surfaces of the d-orbitals.

d-orbital splitting

The five orbitals in an isolated gaseous ion all have the same energy. Because d-orbitals are at the periphery of the ion, however, in the solid state or in solution the energies of the various d-orbitals of the metal ion are affected by the arrangement of the surrounding ions. The overall result is to increase the total energy of the five d-orbitals and, further, to cause a split between the energies of the different d-orbitals. In general terms the orbitals which are closest to the metal–ligand axes and experience the greatest interaction with the negative charge on the ligand will be of higher energy, and the orbitals which are directed away from the metal–ligand axes will be of lower energy. The pattern of energy levels of the d-orbitals will obviously depend on the stereochemistry of the complex ion. The splitting pattern produced by three different configurations is shown in Fig. 9.

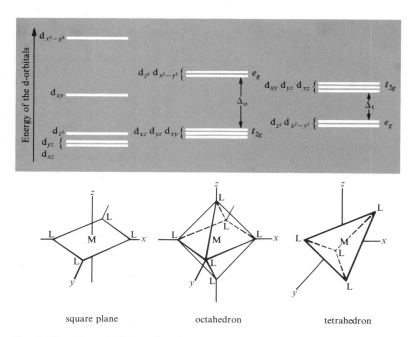

FIG. 9. The effect of different ligand arrangements on the energy of the d-orbitals.

In terms of the octahedral configuration the d-electrons are placed successively in the lowest-energy orbitals first, so that with the d^4 configuration the fourth electron may be placed in one of the higher-energy orbitals, to give

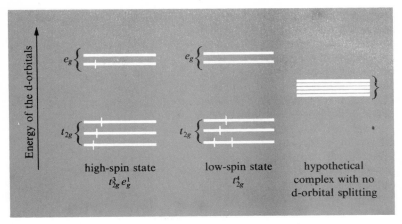

FIG. 10. High-spin and low-spin states of the d^4 ion.

four unpaired electrons. Alternatively the electron may be placed in one of the lower-energy orbitals, already singly occupied, producing one pair of electrons and two unpaired electrons, as shown in Fig. 10. The former configuration with maximum number of unpaired electrons is known as the *high-spin* state, the other configuration is known as the *low-spin* state. Which configuration is adopted will depend on the balance between the splitting energy Δ_0 and the pairing energy P. When $\Delta_0 < P$ the high-spin state will be formed, when $\Delta_0 > P$ the low-spin state will be obtained. For a given metal ion the ligands may be placed in increasing order of the size of the d-orbital splitting they produce. For example:

$$F^- < OH^- < H_2O < NH_3 < NO_2^- < CN^-.$$

This order is based on a study of the visible absorption spectra of transition-metal ions complexed with a variety of ligands, and is referred to as the *spectrochemical series*. There are possible high- and low-spin states for the configurations from d^4 to d^8 with the octahedral arrangement of the ligands.

The low-spin state places the d-electrons in orbitals directed away from the metal–ligand axis and leads to an increased effective nuclear charge on the metal ion, binding the ligands more strongly (Fig. 8). Furthermore the occupied d-orbitals are the orbitals suitable for π-bond formation with π-acceptor orbitals on the ligands, so that complex formation with such ligands is favoured by the low-spin state rather than the high-spin state. Metal ions of the second and third transition series have a much greater tendency to adopt the low-spin configuration, partly because of the lower value of the pairing energy in the larger 4d and 5d orbitals. This is reflected in a greater tendency for such ions to combine with acceptor species, compared with the corresponding ions of the first series.

The stability of the t_{2g} orbitals of the metal ion in an octahedral complex is increased as a result of the d-orbital splitting, while the stability of the e_g orbitals is decreased. Each electron in a t_{2g} orbital will have an additional stabilization energy, so that other factors such as oxidation state being unchanged, the extra stability of, for example, the configuration t_{2g}^3 compared with t_{2g}^2 will make a contribution to the overall stability of the complex. The

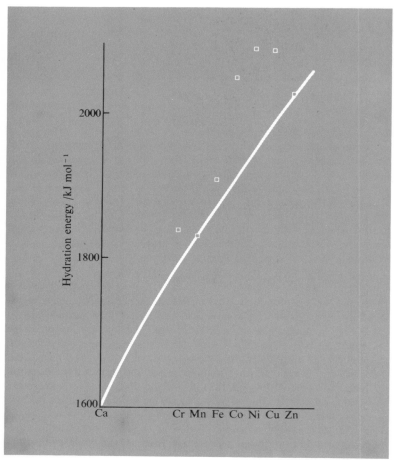

FIG. 11. Hydration energies of M^{2+} ions in the first transition series.

stability of the M^{2+} aquo-complexes will depend upon the hydration energies of the $M^{2+}(g)$ ion, and the non-uniform trend in hydration energies shown in Fig. 11 can be interpreted in terms of additional stability arising from the t_{2g}^n configuration.

Oxidation states

At the beginning of the transition series the ns and $(n-1)d$ electrons are similar in energy, and complete ionization of all these electrons may occur. However, across a transition series the d-electrons become progressively more stable relative to the s-electrons, so although the $ns^0(n-1)d^0$ state is known up to manganese—Mn(VII)—there is no evidence for Fe(VIII), and after manganese the divalent state becomes increasingly stable. This may be compared with the increasing stability of the M^{3+} state from americium onwards in the actinide series.

For many elements of the second and third transition series the M^{2+} cation is unstable, Pd^{2+} and Pt^{2+} being notable exceptions. On the other hand the higher oxidation states show increased stability; for ruthenium and osmium M(VIII) is known (cf. Fe), and even the later members of the series, palladium and platinum, give M(VI) (cf. Ni).

The preference for the higher oxidation states may be compared with the trends in ionization potentials. The first two ionization potentials are very similar for the corresponding elements in all three transition series, but the third and higher ionization potentials are lower in the second and third transition series. Both the 4d and 5d orbitals penetrate the underlying filled orbitals, whereas the 3d orbitals do not, and as a result the 4d and 5d orbitals experience a greater effective nuclear charge. The ionization of the ns electrons, with the resultant increase in charge of the ion, binds the remaining electrons more firmly. For the non-penetrating 3d electrons the increase in effective nuclear charge is more pronounced than for the 4d and 5d electrons. Consequently the binding of electrons in the 4d and 5d orbitals increases less rapidly with increasing charge on the ion. Thus, in going from the first to the second and third transition series we find that the first steps of ionization are comparable but the later steps occur more easily.

Standard electrode potentials

The relative stabilities of the oxidation states of a given element in aqueous solution can be given in terms of the oxidation potentials for the reaction $M(s) \rightarrow M^{n+}(aq) + ne^-$. The successive steps in this reaction may be shown as,

$$M(s) \xrightarrow{\Delta H_s} M(g) \xrightarrow{\Sigma(I.P.)} M^{n+}(g) \xrightarrow{\Delta H_{hydr}} M^{n+}(aq), \quad \Delta H_f = \Delta H_s + \Sigma(I.P.) - \Delta H_{hydr}.$$

The enthalpy changes involved are the heat of atomization of the metal ΔH_s, the total ionization energy for the removal of n electrons $\Sigma(I.P.)$, and the heat of hydration of the M^{n+} ion, with an overall enthalpy change ΔH_f.

TABLE 25

Some properties of selected transition elements

	Ti	Zr	Hf	Mn	Tc	Re	Ni	Pd	Pt
Atomic radius/nm	0.132	0.145	0.144	0.117	0.127	0.128	0.115	0.128	0.129
Total ionization potentials/ (kJ mol^{-1})									
(First and second)	1968	2024	1968	2226	2171	2023	2487	2721	2655
(Third and fourth)	6822	5605	5017	8267	6947	6146	8602	7931	6715
Standard electrode potentials ($E^{\ominus}$/V)									
M^{2+}, M	−1.63	—	—	−1.18	—	—	−0.25	0.98	1.2
MO$_2$, M	−0.86	−1.43	−1.57	—	0.28	0.26	—	—	—

The heat of hydration depends on the size of the gaseous ion and increases across a transition series. The ionization potentials, however, increase to a greater extent and are the dominant factor in the formation of the aquated ions. The heat of atomization increases at first across a series but then decreases. The contribution from this term is most significant for the low oxidation states, when the ionization energies and hydration energies are low. It may be considered the contributory factor to the absence of the M^+(aq) ion. For higher oxidation states the ionization energy and hydration energy both increase, but the heat of atomization remains unchanged, and becomes a progressively less important energy term.

The ions of the second and third transition series are larger than the corresponding ions of the first transition series, and hence have lower heats of hydration. In addition the heats of atomization are also greater for elements of the same group in the second and third series, with the exception of palladium and platinum. Since the first and second ionization potentials are similar for all three series the above factors result in much lower stability of the low oxidation states in aqueous solution. However, the sharp drop in the higher ionization potentials in the second and third series leads to greater stability of the higher oxidation states.

If, instead of forming an aquo-complex, with liberation of the heat of hydration, the ion combines with ligands present in aqueous solution, then the relative stabilities of the two oxidation states will be related to the difference between the heats of complex formation. Certain ligands bind more firmly to the ion in the lower oxidation state, while others bind more firmly with the higher oxidation state. The standard potential of M^{n+}, $M^{(n-1)+}$ will therefore be dependent on complexing species present in the solution. The combination between a cation and an anion to form a complex MX_6^{x-}, leads to an overall loss of hydration and hence an increase in entropy. This effect is greater the higher the original charge on the cation, so that the standard

T ABLE 26

The effect of ligands on the standard electrode potentials of selected transition metal ions

$E^{\ominus}/V$		$E^{\ominus}/V$	
Cu^{2+}, Cu^+	0·15	Co^{3+}, Co^{2+}	1·82
$Cu^{2+}, CuBr$	0·64	$Co(NH_3)_6^{3+}, Co(NH_3)_6^{2+}$	0·1
Cu^{2+}, CuI	0·86	$Co(CN)_6^{3-}, Co(CN)_5^{3-}$	−0·8
$Cu^{2+}, Cu(CN)_2^-$	1·12	Fe^{3+}, Fe^{2+}	0·77
Pt^{4+}, Pt^{2+}	1·1	$Fe(CN)_6^{3-}, Fe(CN)_6^{4-}$	0·36
$PtBr_6^{2-}, PtBr_4^{2-}$	0·64		
PtI_6^{2-}, PtI_4^{2-}	0·39		

potential of M^{n+}, $M^{(n-1)+}$ is reduced. The π-acceptor properties of the ligands do not always increase the stability of the lower oxidation state relative to the higher; rather, certain d-electron configurations are favoured. The t_{2g}^6 configuration occurs in Fe(II) and Co(III) and both are stabilized by CN^-, but the entropy effects stabilize Fe(III) and Co(III). The combined effect results in a greater increase in stability of Co(III) relative to Co(II) compared with Fe(III) relative to Fe(II). Ligands which effectively stabilize low oxidation states in the first transition series may stabilize high oxidation states in the second and third series. For example I^- stabilizes Cu^+ in Cu^{2+}/Cu^+ but stabilizes Pt(IV) in Pt(IV)/Pt(II).

Ion size

The radius of the ion M^{n+} decreases across each transition series, but between the completion of the second transition series and the start of the third transition series there is an additional contraction due to the filling of the lanthanide 4f shell (see p. 46). This additional contraction almost exactly offsets the expected increase in radius associated with the higher principal quantum number of the outer electrons (cf. successive elements in group IA). As a result, for elements of the same group there is a very close similarity between the radii of the atoms and ions in the second and third transition series, and consequently a close similarity in chemistry between corresponding elements in the two series.

Hydrolysis

For cations of the same charge the affinity for water increases across the series, as shown by the increasing heats of hydration (p. 66). The acid dissociation constants of the divalent aquo-ions show a similar trend from Mn to Cu. That factors in addition to charge and radius of the cation are responsible for the hydrolysis of the transition-metal aquo-ions is shown by the trivalent ions from Sc to Co. There is the expected increase in acid dissociation constants due to the increased cationic charge (cf. IIA and IIIA) but there is no regular change with decreasing size of the trivalent ions. It is to be expected that the acid dissociation constant will increase still further with increasing oxidation state, and as the covalent character increases.

The acidity of the metal hydroxides and oxides increases with the charge on the cation, and for a given oxidation state decreases with increasing size of the cation. For the first transition series the hydrated oxides of the divalent ions Co^{2+} and Cu^{2+} will be the most acidic, and they do have weak amphoteric character, dissolving in strongly basic solutions. There is however no evidence for similar behaviour with Ni^{2+}. The earlier members of the series will exhibit increasing acid character in their higher oxidation states; thus Ti(IV) and Cr(III) are amphoteric. For a given oxidation state the hydroxides of the larger ions of the second and third series will be more basic than the corresponding hydroxides of the first transition series.

TABLE 27

Acid dissociation constants (pK_a) for some transition-metal ions $M(H_2O)_x^{n+}$

	Ca	Sc	Ti	V	Cr	Mn	Fe	Co	Ni	Cu	Zn
M^{2+}	12·5	—	—	—	—	10·6	9·5	9·3	8·3	6·8	9·8
M^{3+}	—	5·9	1·7	2·7	5·0	—	2·6	4·8	—	—	—

Solubility

Across each transition series the character of the elements changes from a general resemblance to the pre-transition elements to a resemblance to the B-metals. Thus the cation M^{2+} forms an extensive series of salts with the anions of strong acids, most of which are soluble in water, but salts formed with the anions of weak acids are frequently insoluble. However, the acidity of the M^{2+} aquo-ions is greater than Ca^{2+}(aq) and increases across the series reaching a maximum at Cu^{2+}(aq), so that hydrolysis, particularly of salts of weak acids, becomes more extensive across the series. Thus aqueous solutions of M^{2+} to which weak-acid anions are added will precipitate basic salts; for example manganese(II) precipitates as a normal carbonate but copper(II) precipitates as a basic carbonate.

Divalent cations

The divalent cations give the $M(H_2O)_6^{2+}$ ion in solution, but an increase in the pH favours the formation of hydroxo-species. At pH 6·3, approximately 5 per cent of the total copper in solution is present as $Cu_2(OH)_2^{2+}$ but, under similar conditions, with the less acidic manganese and nickel aquo-ions, less than 1 per cent of the metal ion in solution is present as MOH^+ even at pH 8·0.

The elements of the second and third transition series form very few divalent metal salts. A palladium(II) aquo-ion, $[Pd(H_2O)_4]^{2+}$, is obtained in acid solution, and binary compounds containing Pd^{2+} and Pt^{2+} are known, where the resemblance to group IIB is more pronounced than for the other transition elements.

Trivalent cations

The trivalent ions may be compared in their range of soluble salts with group IIIA; salts with anions of strong acids are generally soluble, and with the increase in charge the M^{3+}(aq) ions will be more acidic than the corresponding M^{2+}(aq) ions. Thus $Fe(H_2O)_6^{3+}$ is present only in strongly acidic solution, and with increasing pH(>2) polynuclear hydroxo-species are formed, similar to those obtained for Cu^{2+}(aq). The salts of weak acids are likely to be very extensively hydrolysed. As already noted the solubilities of the hydroxides show a marked decrease compared with the divalent ions (cf. IIA and IIIA).

The stability of the trivalent cation changes from Ti^{3+} where it is unstable relative to Ti^{4+}, through Cr^{3+} where it is the stable species in aqueous solution, to Co^{3+} where it is so unstable relative to Co^{2+} that oxygen is liberated from the solvent. Thus the chemistry of the trivalent ions may be restricted by such redox considerations. The expected trend in favour of the larger, polarizable anions runs parallel with the increasing oxidizing power of M^{3+}, and there is a greater tendency for complete electron transfer to occur, with oxidation of the anions. Thus iodides and sulphides of Fe^{3+} are unstable in aqueous solutions. Salts of trivalent ions of the metals of the second and third transition series are uncommon.

Rhodium forms a few hydrated salts and the ion $Rh(H_2O)_6^{3+}$ is present in acid solution but iridium does not appear to form an aquo-ion, although a few hydrated salts are known.

Tetravalent cations

In the first transition series there are few salts containing the M^{4+} ions or ions of higher valences. For titanium and vanadium, salts containing oxo-cations are formed, and the higher oxidation states are usually encountered only as the oxo-anions MO_4^{n-}, which may undergo extensive polymerization reactions, as found for VO_4^{3-}. The acidity of the aquo-ion will decrease from the first to the second transition series, and as a consequence hydrolysis will be less extensive. Salts containing the 'zirconyl' ion ZrO^{2+} may be obtained from solutions where Ti^{4+} would be completely hydrolysed. However there is no evidence for an oxo-cation ZrO^{2+} or HfO^{2+}, and salts such as $ZrOCl_2 \cdot 8H_2O$ have been shown to contain the ion $[Zr_4(OH)_8(H_2O)_{16}]^{8+}$. There is little aqueous chemistry of simple salts of the other second- and third-series elements, in this oxidation state or in higher oxidation states.

Complex ions

Divalent cations

The early members of the transition series will be comparable with the pre-transition elements in their preference for particular donor atoms in ligands, and there will be a progressive change with the later elements towards a preference for the larger, more polarizable anions, as found with group IIB. Thus divalent ions from vanadium to manganese have a preference for oxygen donors, and ligands such as hydroxide and acetyl acetonate form particularly stable complexes with V^{2+} and Cr^{2+}, possibly as a result of π-bonding with the d-orbitals. Nitrogen-donor ligands are more firmly bound in the second part of the series, and complexes with ammonia are stable in aqueous solution only from cobalt to copper. For earlier members of the series the additional stability arising from chelation, for example by ethylenediamine, is necessary. The trend towards B-metal character becomes more pronounced with Pd^{2+} and Pt^{2+}, where a wide range of mononuclear complexes $[ML_4]^{2+}$, $[ML_3X]^+$,

TABLE 28

Stability constants ($\lg K_1$) of some divalent transition-metal cations†

	Mn^{2+}	Ni^{2+}	Cu^{2+}	Pd^{2+}	Pt^{2+}
F^-	—	0·7	—	—	—
Cl^-	~0	0·9	0·1	6·1	$\lg \beta_4 = 16$
				($\lg \beta_4 = 15\cdot7$)	
Br^-	—	−0·3	−0·6	$\lg \beta_4 = 13\cdot1$	$\lg \beta_4 = 18$
$EDTA^{4-}$	13·6	17·5	18·8	18·5	—
NH_3	—	2·8	4·3	—	$\lg \beta_4 = 35\cdot3$
			($\lg \beta_4 = 15$)		
ethylenediamine	2·7	7·7	10·8	—	—

† β_4 is the overall stability constant for the reaction $M^{n+} + 4L \rightleftharpoons ML_4^{n+}$, for which the step-wise formation constants are K_1, K_2, K_3, and K_4, so that $\beta_4 = K_1 \cdot K_2 \cdot K_3 \cdot K_4$. Stepwise formation constants usually decrease in the order $K_1 > K_2 > K_3 > K_4$, and so from a value of β_4 a minimum value of K_1 can be estimated for purposes of comparison.

$[MLX_3]^-$, and $[MX_4]^{2-}$ is known, in which the metal ion behaves as a soft acid. Aqueous solutions of Pd(II) or Pt(II) are conveniently prepared as solutions of the MCl_4^{2-} ion.

Certain metal-ion complexes will have an increased stability arising from the d-electron configuration, where the ligand produces a change from the high-spin state of the aquo-ion to the low-spin state in the complex (p. 65). The position in the spectrochemical series at which low-spin complexes are obtained will vary from one metal ion to another, and will also depend on the charge on the metal ion. Since the formation of complexes in aqueous solution involves the replacement of H_2O in the aquo-ion, it should be noted that ligands lying to the right of water in the series (see p. 65) will have an increasing tendency to produce low-spin complexes, with consequent increases in stability. The formation of low-spin complexes by only certain ions of a series may lead to divergence from the pattern of behaviour expected if the ions had formed only high-spin complexes. Because of the progressive nature of the spectrochemical series it is not surprising to find with certain complexes, for example of Ni(II) or Co(II), that the difference in energy between the high- and the low-spin states is comparable with thermal energies, and thus an equilibrium mixture will exist in solution.

Trivalent cations

The stability of complexes of the trivalent metal ions shows a similar trend to that of the divalent ions, so that the approximate order of stability is $Co^{3+} > Fe^{3+} > Cr^{3+} > Ti^{3+}$. Cr^{3+} and Co^{3+} in particular form a very wide range of complex species. These trivalent ions, with the exception of

TABLE 29

Stability constants (lg K_1) of some transition-metal cations in valence states higher than two

	TiO^{2+}	Zr^{4+}	VO^{2+}	Cr^{3+}	Fe^{3+}	Rh^{3+}
F^-	> 5·9	9·8	3·2	5·2	5·2	—
Cl^-	—	1·0	—	0·6	1·5	2·5
Br^-	—	—	—	−3·0	0·6	14
$EDTA^{4-}$	18	20	—	—	24	—
SO_4^{2-}	2·4	3·8	2·5	—	2·0	—

Co^{3+}, have a greater affinity for OH^- than for ammonia, so the hydroxides are precipitated by aqueous ammonia. The stability of the halide complexes is in the order $F^- > Cl^- > Br^- > I^-$ as found for Ga(III), but with the cations of the second and third series the order is $I^- > Br^- > Cl^- > F^-$, as found for Tl(III). One important feature of complex formation is the stabilization of the M^{3+} ion relative to the M^{2+}. This is particularly pronounced with Co^{3+} where a wide range of complex species, stable in aqueous solutions, can be prepared, whereas the simple aquo-ion is unstable (see Table 26).

Higher valence cations

The higher valence states of the first transition series show a marked preference for oxygen and halogen donors. The commonly encountered species are the oxo-anions MO_4^{n-} and the MX_6^{n-} halide complexes. Although an increase in B-metal character is to be expected down a group when going from the first transition series to the second and third series, the stable complexes are still obtained with oxygen and halogen donors ($F^- > Cl^- > Br^- > I^-$) for the first members of the second and third series, and similarly the high oxidation states of all the transition elements form stable complexes with these donor atoms. However, across the second and third series, for a given oxidation state, complexes with the larger, more polarizable anions become increasingly stable.

Stereochemistry

The divalent transition-metal ions differ from the group IIA cations in the variety of stereochemistries which occur. There is a change in the preferred coordination number from six with the early members of the series to four with the later members. The difference in energy between one stereochemistry and another may be sufficiently small for an equilibrium mixture to exist. Possibly the greatest variety of equilibria is found with Ni(II), where in addition to an equilibrium between 4- and 6-coordinate complexes, an equilibrium is found between square-planar and tetrahedral complexes. Palladium(II) and platinum(II) differ from nickel(II) in that tetrahedral complexes are unknown, and there is no evidence for any stereochemical equilibria.

High coordination numbers are encountered mainly in the first half of the second and third series in such complex ions as ZrF_8^{4-} and $Mo(CN)_8^{4-}$, but with the later members of the series the maximum coordination number is six.

Oxo-cations

The oxo-cations of the transition metals are of the general form $MO_x^{(n-2x)+}$, where $n = 3, 4, 5$, or 6; $x = 1, 2$, or 3 and $n > 2x$. The sequence continues through the oxides, when $n = 2x$, and into the oxo-anions when $x = 4$ and $n < 2x$. The oxo-cations are found most frequently with the amphoteric cations, so that the cation MO^{2+} is known for titanium but becomes less well defined with the other larger and more basic M^{4+} cations in the group. In the next group the oxo-cations are well defined for the element in the second transition series, but less well defined for the third transition series. The M^{6+} ion gives an acidic oxide when $M = Cr$, so that it is only the heavier members of the group which are amphoteric and form oxo-cations, such as UO_2^{2+}. Table 30 lists some examples of transition-metal compounds which contain oxo-cations.

TABLE 30

Compounds containing transition-metal oxo-cations

$VOCl_2$	$MoOCl_2$	$ReOCl_4^{2-}$	$RuO_2Cl_4^{2-}$	$OsO_4Cl_2^{2-}$
$VOSO_4$	WO_2Cl_2	$ReO_2(CN)_4^{2-}$		$OsO_4(CN)_2^{2-}$

The pattern of behaviour of the oxo-cations across the transition series is comparable with the behaviour of simple cations. In the early groups the oxo-cations have a greatest affinity for F^-, OH^-, and oxo-anions; examples are $VOSO_4$ and $NbOF_5^{2-}$. Across each transition series the oxo-cations form complexes with more polarizable ligands such as CN^-, NO_2^-, and Cl^- in $OsO_4X_2^{2-}$ and $OsO_2X_4^{2-}$, and N^{3-} in OsO_3N^-. The B-metal character increases still further across the transition series, until the affinity for polarizable ligands is sufficiently large to lead to the exclusion of weakly polarizable donors such as oxygen. Thus palladium(IV) and platinum(IV) oxo-cations are not formed, but complexes of the type $[Pt(CN)_6]^{2-}$, $[PdBr_6]^{2-}$, and $[Pt(NH_3)_6]^{4+}$ are.

Oxo-anions

The transition metals of the first series form oxo-anions of the general form MO_4^{n-}, in which they show some resemblance to the typical elements of the same group of the periodic table. This is particularly true for the elements

Ti $\rightarrow$ Mn (i.e. the elements of groups IVA $\rightarrow$ VIIA) which may be compared with Si $\rightarrow$ Cl (i.e. the elements of groups IVB $\rightarrow$ VIIB). The transition metal oxides are usually weaker acids but stronger oxidizing agents than the typical element oxides. The oxo-anions of the second and third transition series are weaker acids than the corresponding anions of the first series. As already described (p. 32) the weak acids have the greatest tendency to polymerize. The polymerization of the oxo-anions of the transition metals apparently involves a different mechanism, since solutions containing only tetrahedral MoO_4^{2-} species polymerize to give linked octahedral units. In acid solution protonation of MoO_4^{2-} gives MoO_3OH^-, a reaction that occurs more readily for a weak acid oxo-anion. Coordination of water may now occur to give $MoO(OH)_5^-$, followed by dimerization of this species to give

$$[(HO)_4OMo-O-MoO(OH)_4]^{2-}.$$

Further polymerization produces species which contain octahedra with shared corners and shared edges (but not shared faces). The size of the metal ion in the MO_4 unit is of importance, because with decreasing size the radius-ratio effects will not allow six-coordination. Thus ReO_4^- does not polymerize and OsO_4 and RuO_4 can be distilled from acidified solutions of osmium and ruthenium after strong oxidation.

PROBLEMS

8.1. Explain why the standard electrode potential of Co^{3+}, Co^{2+} is changed when the hexammine complexes are formed (see Table 26).

8.2. The third ionization potentials of Cr, Mn, and Fe are 3056, 3251, and 2956 kJ mol^{-1} respectively. Comment on this relative order. What effect will this have on the reducing properties of the M^{2+}(aq) ion in acid solution?

8.3. Comment on the following observations. Addition of aqueous ammonia to (a) a solution containing Ti(IV) gives a white precipitate, (b) a solution containing Mn(II) gives a white precipitate that darkens on standing, (c) a solution containing Cu(II) gives a blue precipitate that is soluble in excess of the reagent.

8.4. Explain the relative order of the standard electrode potentials M^{2+}, M for Ni, Pd, and Pt in Table 25.

8.5. The equilibrium $2Fe^{3+} + 2I^- \rightleftharpoons 2Fe^{2+} + I_2$ is displaced to the right by excess I^- but displaced to the left by added F^-. Comment on these observations.

9. The non-metals

Ionic species

THE elements considered in this chapter are the non-metals, and include the following elements:

$$\begin{array}{ccccc} B & C & N & O & F \\ & Si & P & S & Cl \\ & Ge & As & Se & Br \\ & & & Te & I \end{array}$$

There is virtually no simple cationic chemistry of these non-metallic elements, although down each group there is a trend towards metallic character. For many of the elements there is little solution chemistry of simple anionic species of the type M^{n-}, with the notable exception of the halide ions. All the elements, with the exception of oxygen and fluorine, give oxo-anions of general formula MO_b^{a-}. The elements in the first short period give MO_3^{a-}, while the elements of the later periods give MO_4^{a-}. The tendency to form polymeric units decreases across each period with increasing electronegativity of the central atom (see p. 32). Thus BO_3 and SiO_4 units are found mainly in polymeric linear or cyclic anions, but ClO_4^- occurs only as the discrete anion.

A few cationic complexes are known, particularly in group V, but a wider range of anionic complexes has been prepared, mainly of the type MX_6^{a-} where X is usually halide. The halide and oxide ions form a wide range of complex anions, in which they act as ligand, not as the central atom. In this respect oxygen shows a marked difference from other elements of group VIB, which have less tendency to act as ligands and occur as the central atom, e.g. SO_4^{2-}, $TeCl_6^{2-}$. A similar situation is found in group VIIB, where, although all the ions may function as ligands, only fluorine will not also act as a central atom.

Boron and the group IVB non-metals generally produce oxo-anions in solution which have only the group oxidation state n, that is $+3$ for boron, and $+4$ for the group IVB non-metals. The other non-metals form oxo-anions in a range of oxidation states, including the group oxidation state n, and the $(n-2)$ oxidation state. Consequently there will be a series of redox equilibria for these ions.

Acid properties

The hydrides of the non-metals demonstrate increasing acidity across a period as the following pK_a values show: NH_3 35; H_2O 15·7; HF 3·2. The acidity of the hydrides also increases down a group; thus HI is a stronger acid than HF. These trends may be explained by reference to the following energy cycle with particular reference to the energy changes involved in forming $X^-(aq)$ from $HX(g)$

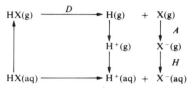

Down the group the decrease in bond energy of $H-X$ more than balances the decrease in electron affinity and hydration energy. Across a period the increase in bond energy is more than balanced mainly by the increase in electron affinity. It should be remembered that small differences in the overall energy change will have a marked effect on the equilibrium (p. 23). All the hydrogen halides except hydrogen fluoride are strong acids in aqueous solution, and it is only in less basic solvents, such as acetic acid, that the acids are differentiated (p. 29) and we find the order HI > HBr > HCl. There is no comparable dependence of the acidity of the oxo-acids on the central atom (see p. 32).

TABLE 31

Energy changes involved in forming X^- from $H-X$

	F	Cl	Br	I	OH
Bond energy of $H-X$, $D/(kJ\ mol^{-1})$	565	431	366	299	464
Electron affinity of X, $A/(kJ\ mol^{-1})$	333	347	324	295	184
Hydration energy of X^-, $H_{hyd.}/(kJ\ mol^{-1})$	515	364	335	297	502

Boron

Boron has a great affinity for oxygen, and the commonly encountered ions of boron are the oxo-anions; many borates occur naturally, usually as hydrates. Simple compounds such as the halides are rapidly hydrolysed. In aqueous solution the complex halides BX_4^- are hydrolysed, with BF_4^- ion having the greatest stability

$$BF_4^- + H_2O \rightleftharpoons [BF_3OH]^- + HF \qquad K = 2 \cdot 3 \times 10^{-3}\ mol\ dm^{-3}$$

Sodium and potassium borohydrides dissolve in water with the formation of the BH_4^- ion and are of importance as reducing agents. Larger anions such as $B_{10}H_{12}^{2-}$ and $B_{10}H_{10}^{2-}$ are remarkably stable in aqueous solution to acids, bases, and oxidizing agents. The insoluble silver(I), and copper(I) salts are formed with no reduction to the metal.

Boric acid $B(OH)_3$ is a very weak acid and strictly monobasic, functioning as an OH^- acceptor, and forming the tetrahedral $B(OH)_4^-$ ion. The acidity is considerably increased by the addition of certain polyhydric alcohols such as mannitol. A chelate complex is produced and boric acid can then be titrated as a strong monobasic acid.

$$\left[\begin{array}{c} HO \\ \\ \\ HO \end{array} \diagdown \diagup \begin{array}{c} O \\ B \\ \end{array} \diagup \diagdown \begin{array}{c} \\ \\ O \end{array} C_6H_{12}O_4 \right]^- H^+$$

Polyanionic species are the major species present in solutions of metal borates and in crystalline borates. The polymeric species contain BO_3 and BO_4 units linked to form rings or chains. Compounds represented as simple salts MB_2O_4, for example, contain long chain anions

$$\left(\begin{array}{c} O^- \\ | \\ -O-B-O- \end{array} \right)_n$$

Boron does give cations of the type $R^1R^2BH_2^+$ in which R^1 and R^2 are ligands with nitrogen-donor atoms such as aromatic heterocyclic amines, aliphatic amines, or ammonia. When the cation contains pyridines and tertiary amines it is unreactive towards water, acids, bases, and oxidizing agents. A three-coordinate cation $4\text{-}CH_3 \cdot C_5H_4N \cdot BCl_2^+$ containing a nitrogen-donor ligand has also been prepared.

Group IVB: carbon, silicon, and germanium

The oxo-species are again the major species encountered in aqueous solution, although silicon does form the SiF_6^{2-} ion, which is the cause of the incomplete hydrolysis of SiF_4;

$$SiF_4 + 2H_2O \rightarrow SiO_2 + 4HF$$

$$SiF_4 + 2HF \rightarrow SiF_6^{2-} + 2H^+$$

One major difference between carbon and silicon chemistry is found with the oxo-anions. Carbon forms the discrete carbonate ion CO_3^{2-}, whereas the ion SiO_3^{2-} exists as polymeric species, usually linear

$$\left(\begin{array}{c} O^- \\ | \\ -O-Si-O- \\ | \\ O_- \end{array} \right)_n$$

Carbonic acid is known only in solution where it exists in equilibrium with carbon dioxide, $H_2CO_3 \rightleftharpoons H_2O + CO_2$. At room temperature 99·8 per cent is present as carbon dioxide molecules dissolved in water, and only about 0·2 per cent is present as carbonic acid. This results in an apparently lower dissociation constant for the acid than the true value $K_a = 2 \times 10^{-4}$ mol dm^{-3} because the bulk of the dissolved material is not present as H_2CO_3. However, it is effectively a weak acid because of the equilibrium with dissolved carbon dioxide, so the salts will be extensively hydrolysed, making it impossible to prepare some metal carbonates from aqueous solution. Only the alkali-metal carbonates are soluble; the group IIA carbonates are insoluble and group III carbonates are readily hydrolysed.

Solutions of silicates and germanates are obtained with the sodium salts. The nature of the species in the solution depends on concentration and pH. In the case of the silicate there is evidence for an extended series of polyanions, but the germanate is less extensively polymerized, and in dilute solutions is present almost entirely as $HGeO_3^-$.

Group VB: nitrogen, phosphorus, and arsenic

There are no simple cationic N^{x+} or anionic N^{y-} species in solution. Complex anions are obtained with oxygen in which nitrogen has a maximum coordination number of three, and phosphorus and arsenic have maximum coordination numbers of four. Nitrates of nearly all the metals are known and are usually soluble in water (see p. 16). Anhydrous nitric acid is both a proton donor and a proton acceptor, so the auto-ionization of the acid may be shown as $2HNO_3 \rightleftharpoons H_2NO_3^+ + NO_3^-$, with the possibility of further dissociation of the cation: $H_2NO_3^+ \rightleftharpoons NO_2^+ + H_2O$. When the pure acid is diluted the more basic water molecule acts as the proton acceptor, and the dissociation in aqueous solution is $HNO_3 + H_2O \rightleftharpoons H_3O^+ + NO_3^-$. The acid is monobasic and often behaves as an oxidizing agent.

Phosphoric acid H_3PO_4 is a tribasic acid and three series of salts may be obtained by successive replacement of hydrogen. Neither the acid nor its salts has appreciable oxidizing activity. The phosphate ion differs further from the nitrate ion in its ability to form linear and cyclic polymeric anions, which are usually obtained as the sodium salts. In solution the linear polyphosphates have the valuable property of forming soluble complexes with metal ions, calcium and magnesium in particular, and are widely used as water softeners.

Arsenic acid H_3AsO_4 is also a tribasic acid, but a weaker acid than phosphoric acid. Polyanions are not obtained in aqueous solution because of ready hydrolysis. Acid solutions have moderately strong oxidizing properties.

$$H_3AsO_4 + 2H^+ + 2e^- \rightleftharpoons HAsO_2 + 2H_2O \qquad E^\ominus = 0.56 \text{ V}$$

$$H_3PO_4 + 2H^+ + 2e^- \rightleftharpoons H_3PO_3 + H_2O \qquad E^\ominus = -0.28 \text{ V}$$

Nitrous acid is a weak acid, $K_a = 6 \times 10^{-6}$ mol dm^{-3}, and aqueous solutions obtained by acidification of metal nitrite solutions are unstable and decompose on heating: $3HNO_2 = HNO_3 + NO + H_2O$. An aqueous solution of nitrous acid functions as an oxidizing agent with reduction to NO, N_2, or N_2O, or as a reducing agent with oxidation to nitric acid. Salts of nitrous acid are obtained with group I and group II cations but there are no nitrites of group III and no simple anhydrous nitrites of any transition metal, except silver.

On the other hand the lower acids and salts of phosphorus and arsenic behave only as reducing agents, particularly in alkaline solution. Phosphorus preserves four coordination by forming P—H bonds in phosphite

$$\left(\begin{array}{c} O \\ | \\ H-P-O \\ | \\ O \end{array} \right)^{2-} \quad \text{and in hypophosphite} \quad \left(\begin{array}{c} O \\ | \\ H-P-O \\ | \\ H \end{array} \right)^{-}, \quad \text{and these ions are}$$

present in the acids and their salts. The P—H bonds are not ionized in solution, so hypophosphorous acid is monobasic and phosphorous acid is dibasic. However the lower acid of arsenic appears to be As_2O_3(aq) although the ion AsO_2^- is found in the majority of salts. It is a weak acid, $K_1 = 6 \times 10^{-10}$ mol dm^{-3}, and only the group IA and group IIA cations form soluble salts.

$$H_2PO_2^- + 3OH^- \rightleftharpoons HPO_3^{2-} + 2H_2O + 2e^- \qquad E^{\ominus} = 1\cdot57 \text{ V}$$

$$HPO_3^{2-} + 3OH^- \rightleftharpoons PO_4^{3-} + 2H_2O + 2e^- \qquad E^{\ominus} = 1\cdot12 \text{ V}$$

$$AsO_2^- + 4OH^- \rightleftharpoons AsO_4^{3-} + 2H_2O + 2e^- \qquad E^{\ominus} = 0\cdot67 \text{ V}$$

Cationic species of the type $(NR_3R')^+$ are stable in aqueous solution, where R = R' = H; R = R' = alkyl; R = R' = aryl; R = H, R' = NH_2; R = H, R' = OH. Salts of the ammonium ion (radius 0·143 nm) generally resemble those of potassium (radius 0·133 nm) and rubidium (radius 0·148 nm) but the ammonium ion is hydrolysed in aqueous solution ($NH_4^+ + H_2O \rightleftharpoons NH_3 + H_3O^+$, $K = 5\cdot5 \times 10^{-10}$ mol dm^{-3}) and solutions of ammonium salts are slightly acidic. Addition of alkali will cause complete decomposition of the ammonium ions, especially if the solution is boiled to remove the NH_3(aq). Ammonia is extremely soluble in water but there is no evidence for NH_4OH. The aqueous solution is a weak base (NH_3(aq) + $H_2O \rightleftharpoons NH_4^+ + OH^-$, $K = 1\cdot8 \times 10^{-5}$ mol dm^{-3}) but the tetra-alkylammonium hydroxides are strong bases. The hydrazinium ion $N_2H_5^+$ and the hydroxylammonium ion NH_3OH^+ may function as either oxidizing or reducing agents.

$$N_2H_5^+ + 3H^+ + 2e^- \rightleftharpoons 2NH_4^+ \qquad E^{\ominus} = 1\cdot28 \text{ V}$$

$$N_2H_5^+ \rightleftharpoons N_2 + 5H^+ + 4e^- \qquad E^{\ominus} = 0\cdot23 \text{ V}$$

$$NH_3OH^+ + 2H^+ + 2e^- \rightleftharpoons H_2O + NH_4^+ \qquad E^{\ominus} = 1\cdot35 \text{ V}$$

$$2NH_3OH^+ \rightleftharpoons N_2 + 4H^+ + 2H_2O + 2e^- \qquad E^{\ominus} = 1\cdot87 \text{ V}$$

Although the potentials indicate strong oxidizing activity the rate of reaction with a number of reducing agents is slow, and the ions are used mainly as reducing agents.

The quaternary salts of phosphorus and arsenic $R_4P^+X^-$, $R_4As^+X^-$, when R = alkyl or aryl, are the only cations of phosphorus and arsenic which are stable in aqueous solutions. These large cations will precipitate large anions such as ReO_4^- and complex anions of metals. Solutions of phosphorus(III) chloride in liquid hydrogen chloride are non-conducting, but crystalline phosphorus(V) chloride dissolves rapidly and the solution process may be represented as

$$PCl_4^+ PCl_6^- + 2HCl \rightarrow 2PCl_4^+ + 2HCl_2^-$$

In non-aqueous solvents the nitrosonium NO^+ and nitronium NO_2^+ ions may be formed. There are no corresponding ions of phosphorus and arsenic. The nitrosonium ion may be regarded as the cation of the weak base nitrous acid $HNO_2 \rightleftharpoons NO^+ + OH^-$; only strong acids react with this base to give salts. Sulphuric acid forms $NOHSO_4$, and the stronger selenic acid gives $NOHSeO_4$ and $(NO)_2SeO_4$. The nitrosonium ion is also present in dinitrogen tetroxide $N_2O_4 \rightleftharpoons NO^+ + NO_3^-$ and nitrosyl chloride reacts with many metal chlorides with the formation of nitrosonium salts.

The nitronium ion is obtained not only in nitric acid but also in solutions of nitrogen oxides in strong acids:

$$N_2O_4 + H_2SO_4 \rightleftharpoons NO^+ + NO_2^+ + 3HSO_4^- + H_3O$$

$$N_2O_5 + 3H_2SO_4 \rightleftharpoons NO_2^+ + 3HSO_4^- + H_3O$$

Stable nitronium salts such as NO_2AsF_6 and NO_2ClO_4 may be prepared but are readily hydrolysed. The nitronium ion present in a mixture of concentrated nitric acid and concentrated sulphuric acid is responsible for the nitration of organic compounds.

$$2HNO_3 = NO_2^+ + NO_3^- + H_2O$$

$$HNO_3 + H_2SO_4 = NO_2^+ + HSO_4^- + H_2O$$

$$C_6H_6 + NO_2^+ = C_6H_5NO_2 + H^+$$

Group VIB: oxygen, sulphur, selenium, and tellurium

There are no simple cationic species in solution, and although simple anionic species such as O^{2-}, O_2^{2-}, S^{2-} exist in the solid state they are extensively hydrolysed in solution. The extent of the hydrolysis decreases down the group,

$$O^{2-} + H_2O \rightleftharpoons 2OH^- \qquad K = 10^{22} \text{ mol dm}^{-3}$$

$$S^{2-} + H_2O \rightleftharpoons SH^- + OH^- \qquad K \sim 1 \text{ mol dm}^{-3}$$

as the acid dissociation of H_2A increases:

Acid dissociation constant	H_2O	H_2S	H_2Se	H_2Te
$K_a/(mol\,dm^{-3})$	4.7×10^{-16}	8.7×10^{-8}	1.9×10^{-4}	2.3×10^{-3}

The soluble sulphides, selenides, and tellurides, formed with group IA and group IIA cations, give basic solutions which are oxidized by air in the order $Te^{2-} > Se^{2-} > S^{2-}$, with the following potentials for basic solution $A + 2e^- \rightarrow A^{2-}$

	O	S	Se	Te
$E_b^{\ominus}/V$	0.4	-0.48	-0.92	-1.14

In aqueous solution the hydroperoxide ion HO_2^- can act either as an oxidizing agent or as a reducing agent (see p. 91). The ion is a poor reducing agent and combines only with strong oxidizing agents; molecular oxygen is always produced when the ion acts as a reducing agent.

$$HO_2^- + H_2O + 2e^- = 3OH^- \qquad E^{\ominus} = 0.88\ V$$

$$HO_2^- + OH^- = O_2 + H_2O + 2e^- \qquad E^{\ominus} = 0.076\ V$$

The commonly occurring ions containing oxygen are the oxo-anions, MO_b^{a-}, of which there are a great number, both monomeric and polymeric. Oxo-anions may also be obtained which contain a peroxo-group and in these circumstances the ion will act as an oxidizing agent, even though there is no overall change in the oxidation state of the central atom in the anion. For example $S_2O_8^{2-} + 2e^- \rightarrow 2SO_4^{2-}$. Both anions contain S(VI), but there is a

peroxo-linkage in $S_2O_8^{2-}$:

$$\begin{bmatrix} & O & & & O & \\ & | & & & | & \\ O-&S&-O-O-&S&-O \\ & | & & & | & \\ & O & & & O & \end{bmatrix}^{2-}$$

. Sulphur, selenium,

and tellurium form oxo-anions such as SO_4^{2-} and SeO_3^{2-} in which they act as the central atom. The oxo-anions of selenium and tellurium are stronger oxidizing agents than the corresponding sulphur oxo-anions.

	Se	Te	S
$E\{M(VI), M(IV)\}$	1.15 V	1.02 V	0.17 V
$E\{M(IV), M\}$	0.74 V	0.53 V	

There is no tendency to form anionic species in which O in MO_b^{a-} is replaced by S, Se, or Te. A possible exception is the thiosulphate ion $S_2O_3^{2-}$, in which the two sulphur atoms are not equivalent, and the ion may be considered as derived from SO_4^{2-} by replacement of O by S. Mild oxidizing agents convert $S_2O_3^{2-}$ to tetrathionate $S_4O_6^{2-}$, a reaction used in the volumetric determination of iodine. The thiosulphate ion forms fairly stable complexes with a number of B-metals, such as Cu^+, Ag^+, and Cd^{2+}.

Sulphur forms thio-oxo salts, containing chains of sulphur atoms; there are no comparable selenium or tellurium ions. The ions may be represented generally as $[O_3S—(S_x)—SO_3]^{2-}$ in which $x = 1–6$. The sulphur in the chains may be readily removed or introduced, and the chains are broken by alkaline hydrolysis:

$$S_4O_6^{2-} + CN^- \rightarrow S_3O_6^{2-} + SCN^-$$
$$S_3O_6^{2-} + S_2O_3^{2-} \rightleftharpoons S_4O_6^{2-} + SO_3^{2-}$$
$$2S_4O_6^{2-} + 6OH^- \rightarrow 3S_2O_3^{2-} + 2SO_3^- + 3H_2O.$$

Sulphur, selenium, and to a lesser extent tellurium form polyanions S_n^{2-}, Se_n^{2-}, and Te_n^{2-} when dissolved in aqueous solutions containing the anions S^{2-}, Se^{2-}, or Te^{2-}. Complex halides MX_6^{2-} are known for selenium and tellurium only. They are hydrolysed moderately easily, selenium more so than tellurium, and are stable only in acid solutions.

Group VIIB: fluorine, chlorine, bromine, and iodine

All the elements form the simple X^- anions in aqueous solution, the ease of oxidation to X_2 increasing down the group

	F	Cl	Br	I
$\frac{1}{2}X_2 + e^- \rightleftharpoons X^-$, E/V	2·87	1·36	1·07	0·54
Ionic radius/nm	0·134	0·180	0·190	0·223

All the halide ions can act as ligands, forming a wide range of halo-complexes. In general with the more electropositive metals the affinity for the halide ion decreases in the order $F^- > Cl^- > Br^- > I^-$. Thus fluoro-complexes are usually the most stable and the metal fluorides the least soluble. However with increasing B-metal character in the cation the order may be reversed, see p. 23.

Polyanionic species are obtained by reaction between a halide and excess halogen. The majority exist only in the solid phase but a few are stable in solution, of which the most familiar is probably I_3^-, obtained when iodine is added to potassium iodide solution. The stability constants in aqueous solution at 25°C for the reaction $AB + B^- \rightleftharpoons AB_2^-$ are:

	Cl_3^-	Br_3^-	ICl_2^-	IBr_2^-	I_3^-
$K/(mol^{-1} dm^3)$	10^{-2}	17·8	$1·6 \times 10^2$	$3·7 \times 10^2$	$7·25 \times 10^2$

All the elements form oxo-anions, with the exception of fluorine. There is no tendency for the oxo-anions to form polymeric species. One important feature of the chemistry of the halogen oxo-acids is the marked tendency to act as oxidizing agents. The acids are much stronger oxidizing agents than are the corresponding anions in basic medium. Also the hydration energies of the acidic oxides increase with increasing oxidation state; as a result the aqueous

TABLE 32

Standard electrode potentials ($E^{\ominus}/V$) of the halogen oxo-anions

Acid solution	Cl	Br	I
HOX, X_2	1·63	1·59	1·45
HXO_2, X_2	1·64	—	—
XO_3^-, X_2	1·47	1·52	1·20
XO_4^-, X_2	1·42	(a)	1·34
Basic solution			
XO^-, X^-	0·89	0·76	0·49
XO_2^-, X^-	0·78	—	—
XO_3^-, X^-	0·63	0·61	0·26
XO_4^-, X^-	0·56	(a)	0·39

(a) Described as a sluggish oxidant, intermediate in apparent oxidizing power between perchlorate and periodate.

solutions (i.e. the acids) will be weaker oxidizing agents than the corresponding anhydrous oxides. Note also that the oxidizing power of the anion decreases with increase in oxidation state of X.

In aqueous alkali the halogens form X^-, XO^-, and XO_3^- (except fluorine which forms F^- and OF_2 only). The products of the reaction are controlled by reaction rates since the equilibrium constants for the formation of XO^- and XO_3^- are large. Thus ClO^- is obtained below 75°C, and BrO^- below room temperature, but above these temperatures XO_3^- is the main product; IO_3^- is the only product with iodine, IO^- being unknown in aqueous solution.

TABLE 33

Stability constants ($lg\ K$) for the reactions shown

	Cl	Br	I
$X_2 + 2OH^- \rightleftharpoons X^- + XO^- + H_2O$	15·87	8·30	1·48
$3XO^- \rightleftharpoons 2X^- + XO_3^-$	27·0	15·0	20·0

In weakly coordinating solvents bromine and iodine give polyatomic cations of the form X_n^+, where $n = 2, 3$, or 5. For example the blue solution produced when iodine is dissolved in concentrated sulphuric acid is attributed to the presence of I_2^+. In strongly coordinating solvents, such as pyridine, cations of the form $(Ipy_2)^+$ are obtained, as are the corresponding $(Br\,py_2)^+$ and $(Cl\,py_2)^+$ ions.

Pseudohalogens

There is a group of inorganic species, each containing two or more different atoms, which have a number of properties in common with the halogen atoms. The most important are CN, SCN, NCO, and N_3, and with the exception of N_3 they form volatile dimeric species, e.g. $(CN)_2$. Single charged anionic species, such as CN^-, are produced, which are stable in aqueous solution but are precipitated by Ag^+, Hg^+, or Pb^{2+} ions. All the pseudohalogens form acids of the form HCN which are usually weaker than the halogen acids. The anions form complexes with a wide range of metal ions, and with some metal ions stable complexes are formed where the corresponding halide complex is unknown, such as $Fe(CN)_6^{4-}$.

Solvated electrons

All the alkali and alkaline-earth metals dissolve in liquid ammonia with the formation of intensely blue coloured solutions. Similar solutions may be obtained with certain amines and ethers as solvents, but hydrogen is evolved with alcohols and evolved vigorously with water. These observations may be explained in terms of three equilibria

$$M \rightleftharpoons M^+(solv) + e^-(solv) \tag{1}$$

$$e^-(solv) + e^-(solv) \rightleftharpoons e_2^{2-}(solv) \tag{2}$$

$$2e^-(solv) + 2M^+(solv) \rightleftharpoons M_2(solv) \tag{3}$$

The metals which give these solutions have large negative electrode potentials in aqueous solution and reaction (1) will be more favourable with these metals. Reaction (2) governs the stability of the solutions. If it is far to the right, as in water and alcohols, and $e_2^{2-}(solv)$ readily form hydrogen gas, then $e^-(solv)$ is highly unstable. In liquid ammonia the $e_2^{2-}(solv)$ species is only observed at concentrations above 10^{-2}M, whereas reaction (2) occurs in irradiated water at concentrations below 10^{-6}M. A solvent of lower permittivity will favour displacement of reaction (1) to the left and reaction (3) to the right; this is in accord with the observed properties of the solutions.

The reaction of sodium with water is shown classically as

$$Na + H_2O \rightarrow Na^+ + OH^- + H\cdot \tag{4}$$

and hydrogen is produced via H· atoms, and not via $e_2^{2-}(solv)$. This allows a possible distinction between the two reactions by the addition of a third molecule such as N_2O which has different rates of reaction with $e^-(aq)$ and H·. The manner in which hydrogen evolution is inhibited has been interpreted in terms of the solvated electron as an intermediate.

The hydrated electron is obtained by radiolysis of pure deaerated water with a pulse of high-energy electrons† and in neutral water it has a half life

† See, for example, G. Hughes: *Radiation chemistry* (OCS 6).

$t_{\frac{1}{2}}$ of 300 μs. The hydrated electron is the conjugate base of the hydrogen atom $H\cdot \rightleftharpoons e^-(solv)+H^+$ and is the more strongly reducing; $E = \sim 2.67$ V for $e^-(solv)$, $E = 2.1$ V for $H\cdot$ atom. The hydration energy of the hydrated electron is calculated as -166 kJ mol^{-1} which may be compared with -297 kJ mol^{-1} for I^-. This suggests a large effective radius of the charge, of the order 0.25–0.30 nm compared with 0.223 nm for I^-, and is interpreted in terms of spreading of the charge over the surrounding solvent molecules.

All the reactions of solvated electrons are reductions, since they involve electron attachment. Some of the reactions are extremely rapid, and generally the reactions are faster than those of $H\cdot$ atoms. Ions with potentials higher than 2.7 V will not be reduced, but other ions and complex ions will be, the nature of the ligands affecting the rate of reaction. In liquid ammonia polyanionic species may be prepared from the heavy metal cations; thus $Pb^{2+} \rightarrow Pb_9^{4-}$. Low oxidation states of metals may also be obtained; thus

$$Ni(CN)_4^{2-} + 2e^- \rightarrow Ni(CN)_4^{4-}.$$

PROBLEMS

9.1. The solubility of iodine in water is 1.34×10^{-3} mol dm^{-3}. In a solution containing 10^{-2} mol dm^{-3} of potassium iodide and saturated with iodine the concentration of iodine is 6.3×10^{-3} mol dm^{-3}, as determined by titration. What is the formation constant of I_3^-?

9.2. Phosphine (PH$_3$) is less soluble than ammonia in water, and the aqueous solution is neutral. Comment on these observations.

9.3. For the NH$_4^+$ ion $K_a = 5.5 \times 10^{-10}$ mol dm^{-3}. What is the pH of an aqueous solution containing 0.1 mol dm^{-3} of ammonium sulphate?

9.4. What are the products of the reactions between the following reagents?
(a) Cyanogen and aqueous potassium hydroxide.
(b) Thiocyanogen and aqueous sodium thiosulphate.
(c) Potassium thiocyanate and aqueous silver nitrate.

9.5. An aqueous solution of borax (Na$_2$B$_4$O$_7$·10H$_2$O) can be titrated against hydrochloric acid. Boric acid may be titrated against sodium hydroxide in the presence of mannitol. Explain these observations.

9.6. Given the electrode potentials on p. 83, what reaction would you expect when sulphur dioxide is bubbled through an acid solution containing TeCl$_6^{2-}$?

10. Reactions of ions in solution

THE reactions of the metal cations considered in the previous chapters have shown that the magnitude of the interaction between a metal ion and an anion depends primarily on the position of the metal ion in the periodic table. Since solubility will in general decrease as the strength of (attractive) interaction between a cation and an anion increases, it follows that a given anion may be used to precipitate certain metal ions in the presence of other metal ions which do not interact as strongly with the anion. This principle forms the basis for the separation of a mixture of metal ions, and is used in qualitative analysis. One reaction scheme for separating the cations in an unknown mixture into groups is shown in Fig. 12.

In selecting a precipitating anion it is desirable that the cation also necessarily added will not be confused, at a later stage in the analysis, with those cations originally present. Precipitating anions are therefore usually added as acids or as ammonium salts, because both the ammonium ion and the hydronium ion may be selectively detected in preliminary tests even in the presence of a mixture of cations. It must also be possible to remove excess reagent from the solution easily after precipitation is complete, and so avoid possible interference with later reactions.

Group separations

The first reagent added to the solution of cations is hydrochloric acid, in which the effective precipitating agent is the polarizable Cl^- ion. Although a number of cations have an affinity for chloride ion only a limited number have a polarizing power which is great enough to form a precipitate and yet not sufficient to form a soluble chloro-complex. Thus Ag^+ and Hg_2^{2+} are precipitated but Au^{3+} and Hg^{2+} form chloro-complexes. The precipitate obtained at this stage constitutes analytical group 1. Once the precipitate is removed, the cations which it contains may be separated further. Thallium and lead in their lower oxidation states show a tendency towards pre-transition metal behaviour, so their chlorides have higher solubility products, and dissolve in hot water. In this group only Ag^+ forms an ammine complex with aqueous ammonia and redissolves, while Hg_2^{2+} forms a black precipitate

$$Hg_2Cl_2 + 2NH_3 \rightarrow Hg(black) + HgNH_2Cl + NH_4Cl.$$

The aqueous ammonia will also dissolve the acidic tungsten(VI) hydroxide which is precipitated at very low pH (p. 22).

The acid filtrate after removal of analytical group I is saturated with hydrogen sulphide ($0.1M\ H_2S(aq)$), in which the effective reagent is the highly

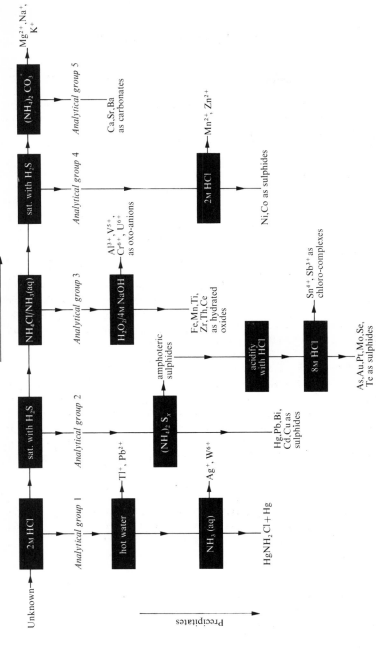

FIG. 12. Outline flow sheet for separation of cations.

polarizable S^{2-} ion. Unlike Cl^-, which is the anion of a strong acid, S^{2-} is the anion of a weak dibasic acid and its concentration is therefore heavily dependent on the pH of the solution. When the solution is approximately 0·5M in

$$H_2S(aq) + 2H_2O \rightleftharpoons 2H_3O^+(aq) + S^{2-}(aq) \qquad K = 1\cdot0 \times 10^{-21} \, mol^2 \, dm^{-6}$$

acid with a cation concentration of about 0·05M, the effective S^{2-} concentration is only 4×10^{-22}M (or one sulphide ion in about 4 ml of solution). So the maximum solubility product of a sulphide that will be precipitated is 2×10^{-23} $mol^2 \, dm^{-6}$. In spite of this requirement a large number of strongly polarizing cations will be precipitated at this stage. The first-row transition elements (with the exception of copper) are not precipitated under these conditions.

The cations which give insoluble sulphides in acid solution constitute analytical group 2, and this group may be subdivided by redissolving some of the cations as complex sulphides. A comparison may be made with the group 1 separation where certain metal chlorides remained in solution as chlorocomplexes. The amphoteric behaviour of the sulphides is also comparable to the amphoteric behaviour of the oxides. Thus the acidities of the sulphides of a given cation will increase with the oxidation state of the cation. The amphoteric sulphides are therefore dissolved in a solution containing polysulphide ions, which act both as oxidizing agent and as complexing agent. Thus SnS has little amphoteric character, but after oxidation SnS_2 readily forms SnS_3^{2-}. After filtering off the insoluble sulphides the amphoteric sulphides may be reprecipitated by addition of dilute hydrochloric acid. Some further separation of this subgroup may be achieved by boiling the precipitate with concentrated hydrochloric acid. Tin(IV) and antimony(III) dissolve as chloro-complexes, since they have a greater affinity for smaller, less polarizable, anions. For example the stability of SnX_6^{2-} decreases rapidly in the order $F^- > Cl^- > Br^- > I^-$, with the bromo- and iodo-complexes rapidly hydrolysed in water. Before proceeding to the next group the excess hydrogen sulphide must be removed.

The next group separation is achieved by precipitation of the metal hydroxides with aqueous ammonia, with the pH maintained at about 7 by the addition of ammonium chloride. These metal hydroxides constitute analytical group 3. Before the addition of ammonia the filtrate from analytical group 2 is oxidized with concentrated nitric acid, with the main aim of oxidizing Fe(II) to Fe(III). The iron is then precipitated as $Fe(OH)_3$ ($K_{sp} = 4 \times 10^{-39}$ $mol^4 \, dm^{-12}$), which is much more insoluble than $Fe(OH)_2$ ($K_{sp} = 7\cdot9 \times 10^{-16}$ $mol^3 \, dm^{-9}$). The earlier members of the transition series in higher oxidation states—such as Ti(IV) and Zr(IV)—will precipitate at this stage, but the later members of the first transition series are sufficiently polarizing to form ammine complexes with the aqueous ammonia and so remain in solution. The precipitate is removed and may be subdivided by extracting the more acidic oxides into sodium hydroxide. As part of the extraction procedure hydrogen peroxide is added to the suspension and the mixture is then boiled. Under these conditions certain metal ions are oxidized to a more acidic state. Thus $Cr(III) \rightarrow Cr(VI)$. The chromium is detected as chromate at a later stage after acidification of the solution. It is important therefore to remove the excess hydrogen peroxide before proceeding to the next stage of the subdivision of analytical group 3. Failure to do this will lead to the reduction of CrO_4^{2-} in acid solution by HO_2^-. A consideration of the two equations shows that although the oxidation $Cr(III)$ to $Cr(VI)$ is favoured in basic solution, the reduction $Cr(VI)$ to $Cr(III)$ is favoured in acid solution:

$$Cr(OH)_4^- + 4OH^- \rightleftharpoons CrO_4^{2-} + 4H_2O + 3e^- \qquad E^{\ominus} = 0.13 \text{ V}$$

$$CrO_4^{2-} + 8H^+ + 3e^- \rightleftharpoons Cr^{3+} + 4H_2O \qquad E^{\ominus} = 1.33 \text{ V}$$

This is one example of the general point that oxidation is easier in alkaline solution and reduction is easier in acid solution. The hydroperoxide ion is one of the few oxidizing agents which are effective in basic solution.

$$HO_2^- + H_2O + 2e^- = 3OH^- \qquad E^{\ominus} = 0.88 \text{ V}$$

The remaining transition elements are now precipitated in analytical group 4 by the addition of S^{2-} to the alkaline filtrate obtained after separation of the group 3 precipitate. Since the equilibrium $H_2S + 2H_2O = 2H_3O^+ + S^{2-}$ depends on pH, with $K = 1.0 \times 10^{-21} \sim c_{H_3O^+} c_{S^{2-}} / c_{H_2S}$, the ratio $c_{S^{2-}} / c_{H_2S}$ will increase from acid solution (0.5 M H_3O^+) to basic solution (3×10^{-9} M H_3O^+) by a factor of 10^{16}, and this is a measure of the increase which can occur in the S^{2-} concentration. The less insoluble transition metal sulphides and B-metal sulphides are precipitated in this group. The precipitate may be divided by redissolving in dilute acid, in which CoS and NiS are insoluble. This is somewhat surprising since these two sulphides did not precipitate under acid conditions. The anomaly is explained in terms of a rapid oxidation of NiS or CoS to Ni(OH)S and Co(OH)S on exposure to air.

The alkaline earths with the exception of Mg^{2+} are precipitated in analytical group 5 by the addition of ammonium carbonate to the filtrate from group 4 which contains aqueous ammonia and ammonium chloride. Carbonate is the anion of a weak dibasic acid, and consideration of the following equations shows that CO_3^{2-} is a stronger base than NH_3

$$NH_4^+ + H_2O \rightleftharpoons NH_3 + H_3O^+ \qquad K_a \doteq 5.5 \times 10^{-10} \text{ mol dm}^{-3}$$

$$HCO_3^- + H_2O \rightleftharpoons CO_3^{2-} + H_3O^+ \qquad K_a = 4.8 \times 10^{-11} \text{ mol dm}^{-3}$$

The CO_3^{2-} concentration is consequently low under these conditions, and $MgCO_3$ will not be precipitated, but Ca, Sr, and Ba carbonates will be. Their solubilities (mol dm^{-3}) are:

$MgCO_3$	1.3×10^{-4}	$SrCO_3$	3.9×10^{-5}
$CaCO_3$	6.2×10^{-5}	$BaCO_3$	4.4×10^{-5}

Still remaining in solution will be the alkali-metal cations and magnesium, which reflects their general solubility in acid and basic solution and their lower affinity for the polarizable anions and the weak-acid anions used as precipitating agents.

Although the scheme of separation has been considered only in outline this should be sufficient to demonstrate one application of the reaction of ions in solution.

The mechanism of oxidation and reduction

The ionic species present in a solution and the equilibria established between them are related to the thermodynamic stability of the various species. However, the usefulness of a solvent may also depend on the *kinetic* stability of the ions in the solvent. In aqueous acid solution (1 M in H_3O^+) the potentials for the liberation of hydrogen and oxygen from the solvent are

$$H_3O^+ + e^- \rightleftharpoons \tfrac{1}{2}H_2 + H_2O \qquad E^\ominus = 0.0 \text{ V}$$

$$\tfrac{1}{2}O_2 + 2H_3O^+ + 2e^- \rightleftharpoons 3H_2O \qquad E^\ominus = 1.23 \text{ V}$$

Thus any couple M^{n+}, $M^{(n-1)+}$ would be expected to liberate hydrogen from water if the potential were less than 0.0 V, and to liberate oxygen from water if the potential were greater than 1.23 V. However, hydrogen and oxygen have overpotentials for their discharge, which means that reducing agents must have potentials somewhat more negative than 0.0 V and oxidizing agents must have potentials somewhat more positive than 1.23 V if reaction is to occur with the solvent. In effect this extends the range over which ions will be stable in the solution; ions may exist in solution which are thermodynamically unstable but kinetically stable. The effect is possibly even more significant for reactions in liquid ammonia where there is a difference of only 0.04 V between the potentials for the oxidation and reduction of the solvent.

$$NH_4^+ + e^- \rightleftharpoons \tfrac{1}{2}H_2 + NH_3 \qquad E^\ominus = 0.0 \text{ V}$$

$$\tfrac{1}{2}N_2 + 3NH_4^+ + 3e^- \rightleftharpoons 4NH_3 \qquad E^\ominus = -0.04 \text{ V}$$

Such a narrow range would mean that very few oxidizing or reducing agents would be stable in liquid ammonia, but the overpotentials for the discharge of hydrogen and particularly of nitrogen again lead to a considerable extension of the range of stable potentials. Kinetic stability of this kind is not found with acid–base reactions which occur rapidly. If a metal ion is thermodynamically unstable with respect to hydrolysis (e.g. $M(H_2O)_6^{3+} \rightarrow M(OH)(H_2O)_5^{2+} + H_3O^+$), then the hydrolysed ion will be formed rapidly.

Oxidation–reduction reactions involve the transfer of electrons from one species to another, and some consideration will now be given to the way in which this may occur. That metal ions exist in aqueous solution as hydrated species has already been noted, with the additional possibilities of hydrolysis, polymerization, or complex formation with the added anion. Two models are recognised for the transfer of electrons between two ions, the *outer-sphere* process and the *inner-sphere* process. The outer-sphere process is required to explain the observation that electron transfer occurs rapidly even though substitution of the ions occurs slowly. Thus MnO_4^- exchanges oxygen with solvent water molecules only slowly and MnO_4^{2-} similarly exchanges oxygen with water only slowly, and yet the transfer of an electron from MnO_4^{2-} to MnO_4^- occurs rapidly. In view of these observations it seems unlikely that the electron transfer proceeds through a substitution stage, with oxygen species acting as electron carriers. It is assumed that an electron is transferred directly from one ion to another. A precondition for such an electron transfer is an adjustment of the Mn—O bond length to a length intermediate between Mn(VII)—O and Mn(VI)—O. This will require energy and constitutes the activation energy of the reaction. After the electron is transferred the Mn—O bond lengths re-adjust to the appropriate length for what are now Mn(VI) and Mn(VI) ions, liberating the energy supplied as activation energy. There is thus no change in the overall energy of the system.

In the inner-sphere reaction, substitution of the coordination sphere of one of the metal ions occurs before electron transfer. In the redox reaction between $Cr^{II}(H_2O)_6^{2+}$ and $Co^{III}(NH_3)_5X^{2+}$ it is found that the anion X^- is always coordinated to the Cr(III) in the products:

$$Cr^{2+}(aq) + XCo(NH_3)_5^{2+} + 5H^+ \rightarrow CrX^{2+}(aq) + Co^{2+}(aq) + 5NH_4^+$$

An explanation is given in terms of a bridged intermediate of the type $(H_2O)_5Cr—X—Co(NH_3)_5$ which facilitates the transfer of the electron from Cr to Co. After transfer the Cr(III) attracts X^- more strongly than does Co(II), and X^- becomes part of the Cr(III) complex. That such a substitution process leading to bridge formation is possible is supported by the rapid rates of substitution observed for the Cr(II) ion. There is one other possibility for electron transfer, and that is the release of an electron to the solvent followed by transfer of the solvated electron to the oxidizing ion. Such reactions occur in liquid ammonia, and are possible with strongly reducing metals in aqueous solution, but there is no evidence to support the idea that these reactions are of general occurrence.

Although two processses are possible for oxidation and reduction it is not always possible to assign a given reaction to one category or the other, and in certain reactions both routes may operate simultaneously. In the presence of Cl^- ions the electron exchange between $Fe^{2+}(aq)$ and $Fe^{3+}(aq)$ apparently follows both the outer-sphere process and the inner-sphere process; both reactions involve $FeCl^{2+}(aq)$ and $Fe^{2+}(aq)$ species. In the reaction between $Co^{3+}(aq)$ and $Fe^{2+}(aq)$ the rate of the outer-sphere process is considerably slower than electron transfer involving the hydrolysed species $CoOH^{2+}$. A similar situation is found with the reaction between $Co^{3+}(aq)$ and $Ce^{3+}(aq)$

where the electron-transfer reaction involves the hydrolysed ion $CoOH^{2+}(aq)$. The equilibrium constant for this hydrolysis has been measured,

$$Co^{3+}(aq) + H_2O \rightleftharpoons CoOH(aq)^{2+} + H_3O^+, \qquad K = 1.75 \times 10^{-2} \text{ mol dm}^{-3}$$

Since the rate of the oxidation reaction depends on the concentration of $CoOH^{2+}(aq)$ it is inversely dependent on the H_3O^+ concentration; the addition of different anions also has a considerable effect on the rate. In the presence of fluoride ion the reactive species is CoF^{2+}, while nitrate ion produces $CoNO_3^+$. The change of reaction rate with change of X^- in CoX^+ may indicate that an inner-sphere process for electron transfer is operating.

Anhydrous chromium(III) chloride dissolves only slowly in pure water, but in the presence of small amounts of chromium(II) it will dissolve readily. This is attributed to an electron-transfer mechanism between the Cr^{2+} ions in the solution and the Cr^{3+} ions in the solid, probably through a chloro-bridged mechanism. After electron transfer the chromium ion in solution will be in the $+3$ oxidation state and there will be a Cr^{2+} ion in the crystal. This Cr^{2+} ion in the crystal is more readily soluble than Cr^{3+}, and once in solution will participate in another electron-transfer reaction with Cr^{3+} in the crystal. The overall process of solution consists of chromium ions dissolving as Cr^{2+}, followed by re-oxidation to Cr^{3+} by electron transfer. The electron-transfer reaction therefore catalyses the solution process.

From these few examples it should be apparent that a knowledge of the possible ionic species in solution is important to an understanding of the manner in which reactions occur. The presence of small equilibrium quantities of complexed or hydrolysed ions may be primarily responsible for the observed rates of reactions represented in terms of simple ions.

As we have already noted, acid–base reactions in water are extremely rapid. The recombination reaction, $H^+ + OH^- \rightleftharpoons H_2O$ is the fastest reaction possible in aqueous solution, with a rate corresponding to the theoretical limit. This theoretical limit is set by the rate at which the ions can diffuse together; the reaction rate is then said to be *diffusion-controlled*. The reaction between H^+ and OH^- in aqueous solution is more accurately represented as a reaction between $H_9O_4^+$ and $H_7O_4^-$ (see p. 5). The hydrogen-bonded nature of these two species allows a rapid rearrangement, leading to the effective transfer of the proton. Thus after diffusing together (a), and forming an additional hydrogen bond (b), the hydrogen bonds rearrange to form part of the water structure. It is this hydrogen-bridged route which effects the rapid transfer of the proton to the electron localized on the hydroxide ion, so that each time the ions $H_9O_4^+$ and $H_7O_4^-$ diffuse together H^+ combines with OH^-. The existence of this hydrogen-bonded path explains why reactions of the hydrated proton are faster than reactions of the solvated electron. The solvated electron is delocalized over a number of water molecules (see p. 87) so the reaction $H^+(aq) + e^-(aq) \rightarrow H(aq)$ is slower than $H^+(aq) + OH^-(aq) \rightarrow H_2O$.

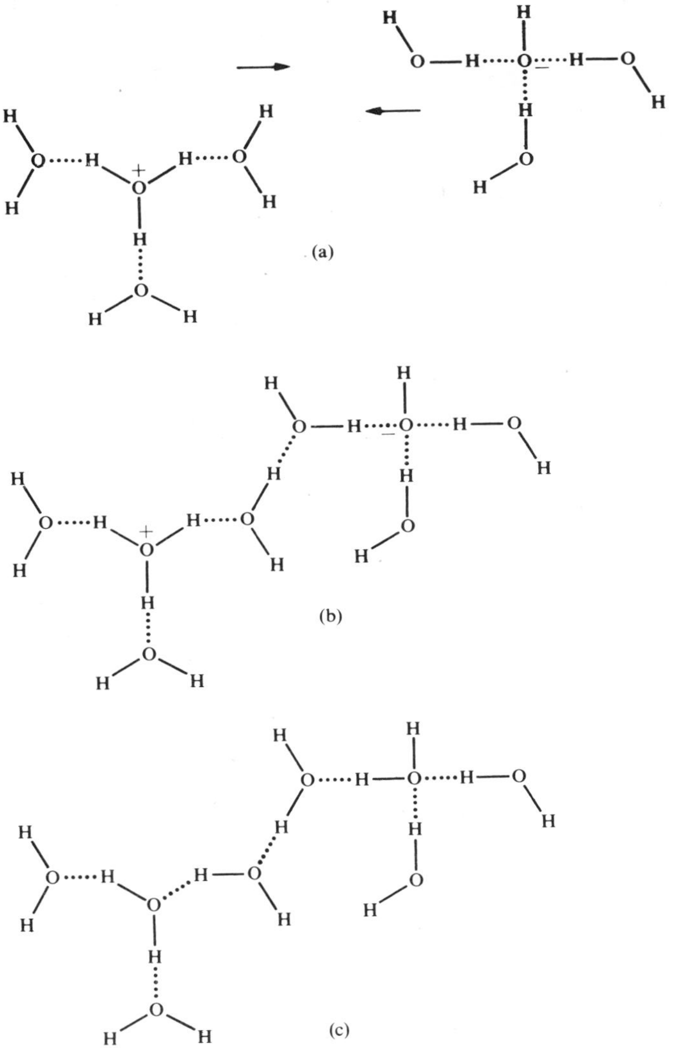

Fig. 13. The reaction between H^+(aq) and OH^-(aq). (a) The ions diffuse together. (b) A hydrogen bond is formed between the ions. (c) The hydrogen bonds rearrange. (..... hydrogen bond, —— covalent bond.)

PROBLEMS

1. Why is aqueous ammonia used in preference to sodium hydroxide to precipitate the hydroxides in group III of the chemical qualitative analysis table?

2. The solubility products of CdS and HgS are 5×10^{-25} and 10^{-54} mol^2 dm^{-6} respectively. Will the metal sulphides be precipitated from a solution in 1M HCl containing 10^{-3} mol dm^{-3} of Cd^{2+} and Hg^{2+}, when the concentration of H$_2$S(aq) is 0.1 mol dm^{-3}? The dissociation constant for $H_2S \rightleftharpoons 2H^+ + S^{2-}$ is 10^{-21} mol^2 dm^{-6}.

3. If Pb^{2+} and Tl$^+$ are incompletely precipitated in group I of the qualitative analysis table, in which later groups would they be precipitated?

4. Sulphide ions give no precipitate when added to a solution containing nickel ions and EDTA. Addition of excess calcium ions produces a precipitate. Explain these observations.

5. Suggest a scheme for the separation of Al^{3+}, Cu^{2+}, Ag$^+$, Cd^{2+}, Hg^{2+}, and Zn^{2+} which does not require the use of sulphide ion.

6. Reduction of Co(NH$_3$)$_6^{3+}$ by Cr^{2+} in aqueous solution is considerably slower than the reduction of Co(NH$_3$)$_5$H$_2$O^{3+}. Explain this observation.

Solutions to problems

2.1. Ca^{2+}, 1520 kJ mol^{-1}; Cd^{2+}, 1535 kJ mol^{-1}.
2.2. (a) $K_{sp} = 4c^3$; $c = 1.35 \times 10^{-5}$ mol dm^{-3}. (b) $K_{sp} = 27c^4$; $c = 1.39 \times 10^{-10}$ mol dm^{-3}.
2.3. $\Delta H_{soln} = 25.3$ kJ mol^{-1}.
2.4. $\Delta G = 55.6$ kJ mol^{-1}; $\Delta H = 66.6$ kJ mol^{-1}.

3.1. 8.7×10^{-7} mol dm^{-3}; 1.40×10^{-3} mol dm^{-3}.
3.2. (a) $K = 1.62 \times 10^6$; (b) Yes; (c) $K = 1.7 \times 10^{-7}$; no disproportionation.
3.4. $K_{sp} = 8.5 \times 10^{-17}$ mol^2 dm^{-6}.
3.5. (a) Hg^{2+} 58.8%; $HgOH^+$ 11.8%; $Hg(OH)_2$ 29.4%. (b) Hg^{2+} 99.8%.

4.2. $K_a = 6 \times 10^{-10}$ mol dm^{-3}.
4.3. (a) 2.37; (b) 4.75; (c) 3.75.

5.3. 1.21×10^{-3} mol dm^{-3}; 7.3×10^{-3} mol dm^{-3}.
5.5. $K_h \times K_b = K_w = 10^{-14}$ mol^2 dm^{-6}; $K_h = 10^{-6}$ mol dm^{-3}.
5.6. Ca^{2+}, 8×10^{-3} mol dm^{-3}; Mg^{2+}, 5×10^{-3} mol dm^{-3}.

6.1. (a) 13.2; (b) 1.82×10^{18}; (c) 2.14×10^{11}.
6.6. $c_{ScF^{2+}}/(c_{ScF^{2+}} + c_{Sc^{3+}}) = 1/(1 + 6.3 \times 10^{-8}) = 1$.

7.1. $K = 10^{16}$ mol^{-4} dm^{12}.
7.3. $K = 1.6 \times 10^{-54}$; no disproportionation.

9.1. $K = 7.35 \times 10^2$ mol^{-1} dm^3.
9.3. 4.98.

10.2. $c_{M^{2+}} c_{S^{2-}} = 10^{-25}$; Hg^{2+} precipitated.

Bibliography

T HE following books each contain one or more chapters which are suitable for supplementary reading.

HARVEY, K. B. and PORTER, G. B. (1963) *Introduction to physical inorganic chemistry*. Addison-Wesley.

SIENKO, M. J., PLANE, R. A., and HESTER, R. E. (1965) *Inorganic chemistry; Principles and elements*. Benjamin.

MAHAN, B. H. (1966) *College chemistry*. Addison-Wesley.

HOLLIDAY, A. K. and MASSEY, A. G. (1965) *Inorganic chemistry in non-aqueous solvents*. Pergamon.

Related books in the Oxford Chemistry Series (Clarendon Press, Oxford)

COULSON, C. A. (1973) *The shape and structure of molecules*.

HUGHES, G. (1973) *Radiation chemistry*.

MCLAUCHLAN, K. A. (1972) *Magnetic resonance*.

PUDDEPHATT, R. J. (1972) *The periodic table of the elements*.

ROBBINS, J. (1972) *Ions in solution (2): an introduction to electrochemistry*.

SMITH, E. B. (1973) *Basic chemical thermodynamics*.

Index

acetonitrile, 61
acid–base reactions, 27, 92, 94
acid, dissociation, 28, 30, 70, 80, 83
   hard, 34, 42, 51
   Lewis, 34
   soft, 34, 56, 57
   strong, 27, 40, 78, 90
   weak, 27, 29, 40, 79, 90
actinide separation, 50
activation energy, 93
activities, 15, 28
alum, 37
ammine complexes, 56, 61, 72, 74, 90
ammonia, liquid, 6, 17, 38, 50
amphoteric behaviour, 33, 41, 47, 54, 61, 90
auto-ionization, 27, 80

base, hard, 34
   Lewis, 34
   soft, 34
   strong, 27, 41, 37
   weak, 27, 54
basic salts, 71
bond energy, 78
   length, 93
Born equation, 13
bridging groups, 42, 93
buffer solutions, 30

catalysed solution process, 94
chelate groups, 49, 72
chloro-complexes, 61
complex ions, 53
   as acids, 30, 50
   disproportionation, 52
   and electrode potentials, 50, 58, 69
complex formation, electrostatic effects, 23, 39, 43, 48, 53
   entropy changes, 43, 69
   with strong-acid anions, 49
   with weak-acid anions, 39, 49
condensation reaction, 22
conjugate pair, 27
contraction in ion size, 70
coordination sphere, 3
covalent molecules in solution, 4, 18

crystal lattice, 3
cyclic anions, 80

detergents, 44
dibasic acids, 81
differentiation of acids and bases, 29, 78
diffusion-controlled reaction, 94
dipole moment, 1, 6
disproportionation, 25, 51, 57

electrode potential, 24, 41, 67
electrolytes, strong, 2, 6, 29
   weak, 2
electron affinity, 53, 78
electrons, high-energy, 86
   solvated, 38, 86, 94
electron-transfer reaction, 93
electronegativity, 1, 32
elution, 49
enthalpy of solution, 11, 17
entropy of solution, 9, 12, 16
   single-ion, 12
ethylenediaminetetra-acetate, 43

formation constants, 23, 48
Friedel–Crafts catalysis, 48

Gibbs free energy, 11, 15, 23
glacial acetic acid, 6, 7, 29

hard acids and bases, 34, 42, 51
heat of atomization, 69
high-spin state, 65, 73
hydrated electron, 87
hydrated-ion size, 40
hydration enthalpy, 12, 54, 66, 69, 84
   entropy, 12
hydrides, acid, 78
hydrogen, atom, 87
   bond, 1, 9, 94
   cation, 40
   hydrolysis, 20, 38, 41, 47, 54, 70, 82
hydronium ion, 5, 88
   in crystalline hydrates, 40
hydroperoxide ion, 83, 91
hydroxide ion, 5
   acceptor, 79

ice structure, 8
inner-sphere, complexes, 3, 39
    process, 93
ion association, 6, 24, 31, 38, 39
ion exchange, 49
ion-induced dipole, 6
ion pairs, 6
ionic product, 28
ionization potential, 46, 53, 67, 69
isomorphous salts, 40, 54

kinetic stability, 92

lanthanide separation, 49
lattice energy, 6, 13
levelling of acids and bases, 29, 31
low-spin state, 65, 73

mannitol, 79
metal ion, basicity, 47
    separation, 88
metal–ligand interaction, 64
monobasic acids, 80

Nernst equation, 25
nitration reaction, 82
nitric acid as solvent, 80
nitronium ion, 82
nitrosonium ion, 82
noble-gas atom, 9
non-aqueous solvents, 6, 7, 17, 29, 38, 50, 61, 80, 85
nuclear charge, 34, 50, 53, 65, 67

octahedral configuration, 5, 37, 44, 64, 76
orbital, 46, 53
    penetrating properties, 67
    splitting, 64
outer-sphere, complexes, 24, 31, 38, 39
    process, 93
overpotentials, 92
oxidation state and acid dissociation, 70
    and hydrolysis, 21, 50
    and oxidizing power, 85
    relative stability, 70, 72
oxides, acidic, 84, 90
    basicity of, 32, 58, 61, 70
    covalent, 32
    ionic, 31
oxidizing agents, 76, 80, 83, 84
oxo-acids, 32
oxo-anions, 72, 75

oxo-cations, 21, 51, 72, 75
oxygen exchange, 93

pairing energy, 65
permittivity, 1, 4, 6
peroxo-anions, 83
pH, 22, 27, 30
π-acceptor ligands, 70
π-bonds, 65, 72
polar effects, 1
polarizability, 6, 72, 75
polarization effects, 17
polarizing power, 6, 21, 42, 46, 58
polyatomic anions, 84, 87
polyatomic cations, 85
polybasic acids, 80
polyether ligands, 39
polymerization, 21, 32, 42, 52, 61, 76
precipitating agents, 88
precipitation, 32, 37, 82
    and pH, 22, 47
pseudohalogens, 86
pyridine as solvent, 85

qualitative analysis, 88

radial distribution function, 34
redox, reactions, 82, 92
    equilibria, 77
reducing agents, 36, 60, 78, 81, 83

size effects, 46, 53, 69, 70
soft acids and bases, 34, 57
solubility product, 15
    salts of strong acids, 40, 47, 54, 57, 60, 71
    salts of weak acids, 40, 57
    trends, 6, 13, 37
solvation energy, 3, 38
solvent, polar, 5
    non-polar, 2
spectrochemical series, 65, 73
splitting energy, 65
square-planar configuration, 64, 74
stabilization energy, 66
steric effects, 43
stereochemistry, 5, 64, 74
strong-acid salts, hydrolysis, 58
structure breaking, 9
sulphide ion concentration and pH, 90
sulphuric acid as solvent, 85

tetrahedral configuration, 8, 37, 48, 64, 76, 79
thermodynamic stability, 92
trivalent ions, stability, 72

water structure, 8
molecule, 1
de-ionized, 44
weak-acid salts, hydrolysis, 47, 57, 71